Contents

Foreword

On behalf of the Medical Commission of the International Olympic Committee I welcome the British edition of the publication Drugs & Sport and congratulate MIMS Australia and Media Medica on their initiative. This reference manual will be of invaluable assistance to doctors, competitors and all those involved in sport who need to know if a medication may or may not be taken. I hope that other countries will follow the lead of Australia and Great Britain and produce their own edition of Drugs & Sport.

Pᶜᵉ Alex. de Merode

Prince Alexandre de Merode
Chairman
IOC Medical Commission

Introduction

Sport is about health and honesty; drug abuse is unhealthy and dishonest and the very negation of sport. Because of the continued misuse of drugs, it has been necessary to strengthen the testing programme in order to 'test out of competition' at short notice or no notice as well as in competition.

I am on record as saying that "only the careless or the ill-advised will be detected at major competitions," hence the need for out of competition testing.

To support the testing programme there is a need for education and information. The International Olympic Committee (IOC) list of doping classes includes substances in common use in medications available on prescription and over the counter.

The publication of a UK edition of Drugs & Sport should provide a convenient reference for the medical profession, coaches and competitors. Whilst it is not intended to interfere with the doctor's choice of medication it will serve as a useful guide to a possible alternative. Nevertheless, competitors have a responsibility to abide by the rules of their sport. Drugs & Sport will be a way to assist them in this endeavour.

Arthur Gold
Chairman
Sports Council Drug Abuse
Advisory Group
and the British Olympic
Association

The Sports Council Doping Control Unit

PLAYING FAIR — NO DRUGS IN SPORT

The Sports Council condemns the use of drugs to enhance performance in sport. Doping can be dangerous, it puts the health of the competitor at risk. Furthermore, doping is cheating and undermines the foundation of fair competition.

The Sports Council is committed to the eradication of doping in sport. All governing bodies in receipt of grants and services from the Sports Council are required to implement doping control procedures and regulations acceptable to the Sports Council.

DRUG TESTING

The Sports Council, advised by its Drug Abuse Advisory Group, has developed an independent testing regime incorporating the following principles:

Independent Testing Under the revised system, events and competitors to be tested are selected by the Sports Council. Governing bodies are invited to make recommendations on targeting of particular events of importance, or of competitors.

Independent Sample Collection Samples are collected by independent sampling officers, trained and appointed by the Sports Council.

Effective Testing Testing is targeted towards particular sports and critical stages of competitive and preparation programmes. Testing out of competition has been introduced and extended to include a wider range of sports, testing at national squad training sessions and of individuals at short notice. Governing bodies are strongly encouraged to include availability of out of competition testing within conditions of eligibility for national squad membership and for international selection.

Penalties Penalties applied must be consistent and effective. The Sports Council recommends a life ban for cases of serious abuse. Results of tests carried out in the United Kingdom are monitored by a Review Panel which is also available to advise governing bodies on appropriate action to be taken, and to advise the Sports Council about the adequacy of doping control measures of particular sports.

SAMPLE ANALYSIS

Samples collected in the United Kingdom are analysed at the International Olympic Committee accredited laboratory funded by the Sports Council, the Drug Control and Teaching Centre.

EDUCATION AND INFORMATION

In support of the testing programme, the Sports Council has launched comprehensive education and information services. A range of education and information material is available to governing bodies of sport and to individuals. In addition, advice and guidance are available to governing bodies who wish to develop their own drug education programmes. A drug information hot-line has been developed to respond to enquiries about banned and allowable substances.

Questions Competitors Commonly Ask

Why is there concern about drugs in sport?

Drugs and other substances are now being taken not for the purposes they were intended, but simply to attempt to enhance performances in sport. It puts the health of the athlete at risk. *It can be dangerous.* It undermines the foundation of fair competition. *It is cheating.*

The only legitimate use of drugs in sport is for medically justified purposes under the supervision of a doctor. Even here medicines should be sought which do not contravene the doping rules and stand no risk of causing harmful effects.

What is being done to control drug abuse?

The Sports Council, in conjunction with the governing bodies of sport, implements a drug testing programme in and out of competition. In support of this there is an education and advisory service, including information on banned and permitted substances.

Who pays for this programme?

The Sports Council subsidises the costs of agreed drug testing programmes. In the majority of cases, the subsidy is 100%.

What is doping control?

It is a system whereby urine samples are collected and tested for banned substances. The aim is to eradicate the abuse of drugs to enhance performance. Where banned substances are found, a disciplinary procedure is followed.

Who will be tested?

One cannot know in advance who will be selected for testing. Selection is made at random on the day of competition or training. Some governing body regulations specify that certain places and events plus a number selected at random will be tested.

How will I know if I am selected?

Immediately after each event, those selected for testing are approached by an independent sampling officer or official of the sampling collection team. If you are chosen, you will have to sign a form to show that you have been notified of your selection and that you agree to attend the Doping Control Station no later than the stated time. Usually, you will be accompanied immediately to the Control Station.

What happens if I refuse to be tested?

Refusal or failure to report may result in disciplinary action being taken by the governing body.

Can someone go with me to the Doping Control Station?

You can ask an appropriate adult to go with you (usually the team manager or other official) but as space is limited, only one person is allowed. Whoever goes with you will not be allowed to witness the collection.

What happens at the Doping Control Station?

The Doping Control Station is a quiet place where the sample of urine can be provided, and is bottled and sealed in the correct way.

You will be required to identify yourself and the collection procedure will be explained. You will then be asked to:

- choose a pair (A and B) of 2 numbered bottles

- provide at least 100 mL (approximately ⅕ of a pint) of urine under supervision
- divide the sample between between the 2 bottles chosen
- seal the bottles with a unique seal
- check that the numbers on the bottles and outer containers have been recorded correctly
- enter on the form any medications you have been taking in the past 7 days
- sign that you are satisfied with the sample collection procedure

What if I cannot produce the required sample?

Don't worry. Plenty of drinks will be available and you will be given plenty of time and encouragement.

What happens to the samples?

They will be sent to an International Olympic Committee accredited laboratory for analysis.

What happens if no banned substances are found?

The negative result will be reported to the governing body and they will inform you. The reserve sample will then be destroyed.

What happens if a banned substance is found?

The governing body will be notified that a particular substance has been found and will then inform you.

Usually the procedure is then as follows:

- you will be invited to provide an explanation of the finding
- you will be given the opportunity to attend or be represented at the analysis of the reserve sample
- you and/or a representative of your choice will be able to present your case at the governing body disciplinary hearing
- a decision will then be taken. Disciplinary action may include suspension from competitions for a specified period or may even be a life ban
- you are entitled to appeal against the decision

What drugs are banned?

The list usually adopted is the list of banned doping classes and methods produced by the International Olympic Committee (IOC) but you should check with your governing body to be absolutely sure. Details of the list are given in the Explanations of Doping Classes and Methods section.

How harmful can taking drugs be?

Taking banned drugs over a period of time can seriously increase the chances of harmful side effects occurring. These side effects have been fatal in a number of athletes.

If I am not taking any drugs on the IOC list, do I need to worry?

YES. The IOC list is not complete. Many common medicines, whether prescribed by a doctor or purchased at a pharmacy, contain banned substances such as codeine, ephedrine, etc.

How can I be safe?

The only completely safe way is to TAKE NO DRUGS. If you need to take medication you should check IN ADVANCE that it does not contain a banned substance.

REMEMBER: THIS IS THE COMPETITOR'S RESPONSIBILITY

How do I check?

A list of banned classes of drugs and substances can be obtained from your governing body or the Sports Council, who should be able to advise you whether a medication is 'safe'. *Remember, your own doctor or chemist may not always be able to tell you whether a drug contains a banned substance.*

IF POSSIBLE CHECK MEDICATIONS BEFORE TAKING THEM

What if I need medicines for conditions such as asthma or hay fever?

There are usually suitable alternative products which do not contain banned substances. Your doctor will be able to advise you in the first instance but REMEMBER...it is strongly recommended that the composition of the medicine is checked against the list of banned substances and with your governing body.

Are herbs banned?

YES and NO! Most herbs are safe, however, some are not. Herbal combinations often contain banned substances such as Ma Huang (Chinese Ephedra), a naturally occurring plant containing the banned substance ephedrine. REMEMBER to check what the herbal preparation contains. If in doubt do not take herbal products.

How long do drugs stay in my system?

This is extremely variable, depending on the drug and the individual. Some drugs can be eliminated rapidly, while for others, traces can remain for several months.

Can I avoid detection?

NO — the drug test is extremely sensitive; even trace amounts can be detected and identified.

Couldn't I fill the bottles with someone else's urine?

NO — an official will be with you to ensure that the sample is collected in the correct way.

Is it worth the risk?

NO! It may damage your health and your future in the sport. In addition, it could endanger the reputation of your sport in this country and abroad.

Sample Collection Procedures

Governing bodies of competitive sport in the UK have rules prohibiting the abuse of drugs.

Because of the serious consequences of proven drug abuse, it is important that participants, administrators, coaches, parents and teachers are all fully aware of the rules and procedures for drug testing, so that their own and sport's interests, can be safeguarded.

The following procedures are used by the Sports Council's Independent Sampling Officers to ensure that the samples are collected in a fair and equal manner and that there is no possibility of a person being falsely accused of having taken a prohibited drug. The competitor must understand the procedure adopted, must have a free choice of the containers available and must be satisfied that the containers holding his/her samples are securely sealed and tamperproof.

These recommendations follow the general guidelines laid down by the International Olympic Committee.

FACILITIES

A Doping Control Station is required to provide the necessary privacy and security. Ideally it should consist of three interconnected areas, one to be a waiting room, the others for administration and sample collection.

The administration room should contain table and chairs, a wash basin, the sample containers, suitable materials for sealing containers, writing material, and a lavatory in an adjacent room. In addition, a lockable freezer or refrigerator for the storage of samples should be available in this room or in another secure area.

The waiting room should have chairs, clothes hangers and hooks, an adequate supply of drinks which must be in unopened containers and possibly some magazines. Entry to the Doping Control Station must be restricted to authorised personnel.

Sports Council Mobile Sampling Units provide suitable facilities when none are available at a venue.

GOVERNING BODY EVENT ORGANISER'S PRELIMINARY ORGANISATION

- Arrangements should be made so that someone is present to liaise with the sampling officers and who has the authority to decide upon any problems which might arise in the collection of samples. This would usually be the governing body's doping control officer who should remain at the Doping Control Station until all samples have been collected.

- Nomination of stewards to assist the sample collection procedures.

- Provision of an adequate supply of soft drinks which must be in individual, unopened containers.

- Arrangements for access to the event for the Mobile Sampling Unit, if being used, together with the provision of a convenient parking place.

SELECTION OF INDIVIDUALS FOR TESTING

Selection is normally made by the Independent Sampling Officer on the day of competition or training session and may be made in conjunction with a senior official of the governing body concerned.

Some governing bodies of sport specify that certain places and events plus a number selected at random will be tested.

Competitors selected for testing will be notified by an authorised official. Those selected will be asked to sign a form to acknowledge that they have been notified and have agreed to go to the Doping Control Station no later than a stated time. Usually they can go to the Control Station straight away and may be accompanied by a coach, doctor or official.

COLLECTION OF SAMPLES

Proper surveillance must be present at all times, but every effort will be made to maintain the privacy and dignity of the individual. At mixed events it is obviously imperative that sampling officers of both sexes are present.

- The time of arrival of the competitor at the Control Station must be noted.

- The competitor must be clearly identified.

- Only one competitor at a time should be allowed into the administration room.

- The competitor must be informed as to how the sample is taken and the minimum quantity of urine (100 mL) required.

- The competitor must be allowed a free choice of one pair from the suitably labelled bottles provided.

- An Independent Sampling Officer of the same sex must accompany the competitor to the toilet and must observe the sample being given.

- The urine sample must be divided normally into two bottles according to the protocol. One bottle will be used for the first analysis and the second bottle kept at the laboratory as a reserve sample should a second analysis be required.

- The pH may be measured using a portion of the urine sample with the suitable test equipment.

- The containers should be sealed and the seal numbers recorded.

- The competitor should be asked to declare any drugs taken within the last 7 days. (A form asking the question in the relevant language would be helpful). Care should be taken to ensure that the competitor understands what a drug is, ie. any substance introduced into the body which is not a food.

- The necessary forms must be completed carefully. When the whole procedure has been completed correctly, a signature should be obtained from the competitor confirming that he/she is satisfied with the procedure.

- The competitor should be given and should retain the bottom copy of the Doping Control Collection form.

- The containers will be placed in an outer transportation bag, together with the laboratory copies of the Doping Control Collection forms.

- The samples must be delivered to the Analytical Laboratory as soon as possible after collection by a secure chain of custody. If any delay seems likely the samples must be placed in a refrigerator and preferably be deep frozen.

- If the competitor refuses to give a sample of urine, the possible consequences should be pointed out. If the competitor still refuses, the fact shall be noted on the Doping Control Collection form and signed by all present.

ANALYSIS OF SAMPLES

All samples taken are sent to an IOC accredited laboratory.

The results of analysis are normally forwarded to the Sports Council within two weeks of the event and to the governing body concerned immediately after.

Should the results be required more quickly, this can be arranged provided adequate advance notice is given. There may be an additional charge for the service which the organising body will be required to pay.

Action on Results

The governing body is recommended to notify all individuals concerned of the results of the drug test even where the report indicated that no substance banned by the Medical Commission of the IOC or International Federation has been detected in any of the samples taken at an event. This should include, if appropriate, individuals and/or governing bodies from visiting countries.

ADVERSE FINDINGS

The existence of a substance or a metabolite of a banned doping class in the analysis of the first sample will be notified by the IOC accredited laboratory to the Sports Council who will immediately inform the governing body of the identity of the individual concerned and the name of the substance detected.

The governing body shall immediately inform the individual of the substance detected. At present, the individual has the right to insist that the reserve sample be analysed to confirm the finding in the first sample and to be present, or to be represented, at the analysis which shall normally be within 7 days of notification.

GOVERNING BODY INVESTIGATION

The governing body shall hold an investigation to which the alleged offender shall be invited.

The decision to initiate disciplinary proceedings because of a possible breach of the doping regulations, including a refusal to submit to a test, should be taken by a properly constituted body with that authority and not by an individual.

Advice and assistance in interpreting the result of the analysis is available from the Sports Council.

SUSPECTED INDIVIDUAL'S RIGHTS

It is important to protect the confidentiality of the suspected individual until a positive case of doping has been declared and a penalty awarded.

Disciplinary proceedings should be conducted before a duly constituted body with that authority and which shall protect the suspected athlete's right to a fair hearing and examination.

The persons bringing the case should be separate and distinct from those who may award penalties.

The suspected individual should be:

- Informed in writing of the case against him/her and provided with all other relevant documentary evidence and material which will form the basis of the accusation;

- Informed of the date and place of the proceedings and given sufficient time to prepare his/her defence;

- Allowed the right to present evidence and to comment on the accusation, or to be represented by a person of his/her own choice with the same rights.

The proceedings should be thorough and impartial; they need not be modelled on civil court procedures and the suspected individual should have the benefit of any doubt.

The suspected individual together with the Sports Council should be informed, in writing, of the decision reached and the reasons.

RIGHT OF APPEAL

An individual found guilty should be informed of his/her right of appeal to an appropriate body empowered to hear such appeals together with the method of lodging an appeal.

The principles for a fair hearing apply also to proceedings of the appeal body and no attempt should be made to deny the individual his/her right, as a last resort, to have recourse to law.

PENALTIES

It is recommended that governing body regulations include a list of applicable and appropriate penalties (fines, exclusions, suspensions, etc) together with provision for assessing mitigating or aggravating circumstances.

To avoid clashes of authority, it is also recommended that governing bodies include a clause implementing the doping regulations of their British/International Federations where these exist.

If detection is to be an effective deterrent, penalties must be meaningful, particularly in every case of blatant abuse by those who cheated knowingly, be they coaches, competitors or administrators.
The Medical Commission of the IOC recommended the following sanction in March 1988 which governing bodies of sport are strongly advised to adopt.

For offences involving:

- ANABOLIC STEROIDS, AMPHETAMINE-related and other STIMULANTS, CAFFEINE, DIURETICS, BETA-BLOCKERS, NARCOTIC ANALGESICS and DESIGNER DRUGS:
    - a two-year ban for the first offence.
    - a life ban for the second offence.

- EPHEDRINE, PHENYLPROPANOLAMINE, CODEINE, etc. (when administered orally as a cough suppressant or painkiller in association with decongestants and/or antihistamines):
    - a maximum ban of three months for the first offence.
    - a two-year ban for the second offence.
    - a life ban for the third offence.

The IOC Medical Commission recommends that before a final decision is made on a particular case, a fair hearing be granted for the competitor (and possibly the other persons concerned).

Such a hearing should take into consideration the circumstances (extenuating or not) and the known facts of the case. During the hearing it is also recommended that the head of the IOC accredited laboratory who reported the result be consulted.

The Medical Commission also recommends to sports authorities that even more severe sanctions have to be taken against all persons other than the competitor involved in the doping case if the guilt of such persons can be unequivocally established.

PUBLICITY OF RESULTS

Once the final decision has been reached and notified to the individual concerned, the result and action should be published by the governing body to its membership.

The Sports Council may publish summaries of the testing, the results, both positive and negative, and the action taken.

Sample Collection Procedures for Young Competitors

Doping Controls are presently carried out at several national competitions at which young children compete, either alongside adults in events run by 'parent' governing bodies or in those run by schools' governing bodies.

SENIOR GOVERNING BODY EVENTS

In those events where juniors compete in senior governing body events, it is important that both competitors and parents are aware that doping controls may be carried out at any time and that, under the rules of the governing body involved, any competitor selected for testing is required to give a sample.

Governing bodies should include such notice on the entry form for competitions, or on the invitations issued to individuals to attend national squad training and/or trials.

PARENTAL CONSENT

Where young competitors are involved, entry and acceptance forms should be signed by a parent or guardian on behalf of the competitor to confirm that the individual understands and accepts the conditions stated, otherwise the entry will not be accepted.

SCHOOLS' GOVERNING BODY EVENTS

Testing may be carried out at schools competitions of certain sports at national level.

Doping control is now a regular occurrence at national and international events. However it can be traumatic for young competitors the first time they are selected for testing, particularly if this happens at an event abroad where the sampling officers may not speak English.

Much of the associated worry can be removed if the competitors are familiar with the procedures involved, and have experienced their first doping control at a domestic event where the sampling officers are sensitive to their needs.

Governing bodies have a responsibility to ensure that all competitors are fully aware of the rules governing drug abuse in their sport, and are familiar with the procedures involved, both for their own and for the individual's protection.

The Sports Council provides, free of charge, advisory booklets on all aspects of doping control, which can be issued to squad members and which will answer most of the questions that children and their parents might ask.

PROCEDURES FOLLOWING A POSITIVE FINDING

If the laboratory reports a positive finding in the urine of a young competitor under the age stipulated by the relevant governing body, the governing body shall inform the competitor's parent or guardian in writing of the substance detected and provide copies of the laboratory data.

The parent/guardian will be advised to discuss with the competitor the finding and will be invited to explain it. The parent/guardian will have the opportunity to insist on the analysis of the 'B' sample and to be present (with the competitor if requested) or to be represented at this analysis. The analysis shall normally take place within seven days of notification. Arrangements for the 'B' sample analysis should be made with the Sports Council.

The competitor may be suspended from competition until the 'B' sample has been analysed and/or disciplinary proceedings have been conducted.

The governing body shall hold an investigation into the circumstances of the finding to which the competitor's parent/guardian shall be invited.

TREATMENT GUIDELINES

In many cases, an adverse finding is found to be the result of the competitor taking a medication containing a banned substance, either bought over the counter or prescribed by a doctor.

To avoid inadvertent contravention of the doping regulations, competitors, their parents, teachers and coaches should be made aware of the rules and advised to follow the treatment guidelines.

CONCLUSION

Governing bodies of all sports which involve young competitors are recommended to give careful consideration to the advice given here.

Doping control should be regarded as an integral part of competing in sport. Young people starting on the sporting ladder will develop a greater understanding of the issues involved, the potential problems and help educate about the dangers of drug abuse in sport.

Explanations of Doping Classes and Methods

Drugs & Sport is based on the International Olympic Committee list of doping classes and methods.

The doping definition of the IOC Medical Commission is based on the banning of pharmacological classes of agents. The definition has the advantage that also new drugs, some of which may be especially designed for doping purposes, are banned.

If substances of the banned classes are detected in the laboratory the IOC Medical Commission will act. It should be noted that the presence of the drug in the urine constitutes an offence, irrespective of the route of administration.

1. Doping Classes

A. Stimulants
B. Narcotics
C. Anabolic steroids
D. Beta-blockers
E. Diuretics
F. Peptide hormones and analogues

2. Doping Methods

A. Blood doping
B. Pharmacological, chemical and physical manipulation

3. Classes of Drugs Subject to Certain Restrictions

A. Alcohol
B. Marijuana
C. Local anaesthetics
D. Corticosteroids

EXPLANATIONS

1. Doping Classes

A. Stimulants

Stimulants comprise various types of drugs which increase alertness, reduce fatigue and may increase competitiveness and hostility. Their use can also produce loss of judgement, which may lead to accidents to others in some sports. Amphetamine and related compounds have the most notorious reputation in producing problems in sport. Some deaths of sportsmen have resulted even when normal doses have been used under conditions of maximum physical activity. There is no medical justification for the use of 'amphetamines' in sport.

One group of stimulants is the sympathomimetic amines of which ephedrine is an example. In high doses, this type of compound produces mental stimulation and increased blood flow. Adverse effects include elevated blood pressure and headache, increased and irregular heart beat, anxiety and tremor. In lower doses, they eg. ephedrine, pseudoephedrine, phenylpropanolamine, norpseudoephedrine, are often present in cold and hay fever preparations which can be purchased in pharmacies and sometimes from other retail outlets without the need of a medical prescription.

Note. All imidazole preparations are acceptable for topical use, eg. oxymetazoline.

Note. β2 agonists.
The choice of medication in the treatment of asthma and respiratory ailments has posed many problems. Some years ago, ephedrine and related substances were administered quite frequently. However, these substances are prohibited because they are classed in the category of sympathomimetic amines and **therefore considered as stimulants**.
The use of only the following β2 agonists **is permitted in the aerosol form:**
bitolterol
orciprenaline
rimiterol
salbutamol
terbutaline

B. Narcotic analgesics

The drugs belonging to this class, which are represented by morphine and its chemical and pharmacological analogues, act fairly specifically as analgesics for the management of moderate to severe pain. This description however by no means implies that their clinical effect is limited to the relief of trivial disabilities. Most of these drugs have major side effects, including dose related respiratory depression, and carry a high risk of physical and psychological dependence. There exists evidence indicating that narcotic analgesics have been and are abused in sports, and therefore the IOC Medical Commission has issued and maintained a ban on their use during the Olympic Games. The ban is also justified by international restrictions affecting the movement of these compounds and is in line with the regulations and recommendations of the World Health Organisation regarding narcotics.

Furthermore, it is felt that the treatment of slight to moderate pain can be effective using drugs, other than the narcotics, which have analgesic, anti-inflammatory and antipyretic actions. Such alternatives, which have been successfully used for the treatment of sports injuries, include anthranilic acid derivatives (such as mefenamic acid, floctafenine, glafenine, etc.), phenylalkanoic acid derivatives (such as diclofenac, ibuprofen, ketoprofen, naproxen, etc.) and compounds such as indomethacin and sulindac. The Medical Commission also reminds competitors and team doctors that aspirin and its newer derivatives (such as diflunisal) are not banned but cautions against some pharmaceutical preparations where aspirin is often associated with a banned drug such as codeine. The same precautions hold for cough and cold preparations which often contain drugs of the banned classes.

Note. Dextromethorphan and pholcodine are **not banned** and may be used as antitussives. Diphenoxylate, an antidiarrhoeal, is **also permitted**.

C. Anabolic steroids

This class of drugs includes chemicals which are related in structure and activity to the male hormone testosterone, which is also included in this banned class. They have been misused in sport, not only to attempt to increase muscle bulk, strength and power when used with increased food intake, but also in lower doses and normal food intake to attempt to improve competitiveness.

Their use in teenagers who have not fully developed can result in stunting growth by affecting growth at the ends of the long bones. Their use can produce psychological changes, liver damage and adversely affect the cardiovascular system. In males, their use can reduce testicular size and sperm production; in females, their use can produce masculinisation, acne, development of male pattern hair growth and suppression of ovarian function and menstruation.

D. Beta-blockers

The IOC Medical Commission has reviewed the therapeutic indications for the use of β-blocking drugs and noted that there is now a wide range of effective alternative preparations available to control hypertension, cardiac arrhythmias, angina pectoris and migraine. Due to the continued misuse of β-blockers in some sports where physical activity is of no or little importance, the IOC Medical Commission reserves the right to test those sports which it deems appropriate. These are unlikely to include endurance events which necessitate prolonged periods of high cardiac output and large stores of metabolic substrates in which β-blockers would severely decrease performance capacity.

E. Diuretics

Diuretics have important therapeutic indications for the elimination of fluids from the tissues in certain pathological conditions. However, strict medical control is required.

Diuretics are sometimes misused by competitors for two main reasons, namely: to reduce weight quickly in sports where weight categories are involved and to reduce the concentration of drugs in urine by producing a more rapid excretion of urine to attempt to minimise detection of drug misuse. Rapid reduction of weight in sport cannot be justified medically. Health risks are involved in such misuse because of serious side effects which might occur.

Furthermore, deliberate attempts to reduce weight artificially in order to compete in lower weight classes or to dilute urine constitute clear manipulations which are unacceptable on ethical grounds. Therefore, the IOC Medical Commission has decided to include diuretics on its list of banned classes of drugs.

Note. For sports involving weight classes, the IOC Medical Commission reserves the right to obtain urine samples from the competitor at the time of the weigh-in.

F. Peptide hormones and analogues

Chorionic Gonadotrophin (HCG - human chorionic gonadotrophin): it is well known that the administration to males of HCG and other compounds with related activity leads to an increased rate of production of endogenous androgenic steroids and is considered equivalent to the exogenous administration of testosterone.

Corticotrophin (ACTH): Corticotrophin has been misused to increase the blood levels of endogenous corticosteroids notably to obtain their euphoric effect. The application of Corticotrophin is considered to be equivalent to the oral, intramuscular or intravenous application of corticosteroids. (See section 3D.)

Growth hormone (HGH, somatotrophin): the misuse of Growth Hormone in sport is deemed to be unethical and dangerous because of various adverse effects, for example, allergic reactions, diabetogenic effects, and acromegaly when applied in high doses.

Erythropoietin (EPO): is the glucoprotein hormone produced in the human kidney which regulates, apparently by a feed-back mechanism, the rate of synthesis of erythrocytes.

All the respective releasing factors of the above mentioned substances are also banned.

2. Methods

A. Blood doping

Blood transfusion is the intravenous administration of red blood cells or related blood products that contain red blood cells. Such products can be obtained from blood drawn from the same (autologous) or from a different (nonautologous) individual. The most common indications for red blood transfusion in conventional medical practice are acute blood loss and severe anaemia.

Blood doping is the administration of blood or related red blood products to a competitor other than for legitimate medical treatment. This procedure may be preceded by withdrawal of blood from the competitor who continues to train in this blood-depleted state.

These procedures contravene the ethics of medicine and of sport. There are also risks involved in the transfusion of blood and related blood products. These include the development of allergic reactions (rash, fever, etc.) and acute haemolytic reaction with kidney damage if incorrectly typed blood is used, as well as delayed transfusion reaction resulting in fever and jaundice, transmission of infectious diseases (viral hepatitis and AIDS), overload of the circulation and metabolic shock.

Therefore the practice of blood doping in sport is banned by the IOC Medical Commission.

The IOC Medical Commission also bans Erythropoietin as a method analogous to doping (see 1.F. Peptide hormones and analogues).

B. Pharmacological, chemical and physical manipulation

The IOC Medical Commission bans the use of substances and methods which alter the integrity and validity of urine samples used in doping controls. Examples of banned methods are catheterisation, urine substitution and/or tampering, inhibition of renal excretion.

3. Classes of Drugs Subject to Certain Restrictions

A. Alcohol

Alcohol is not prohibited. However breath or blood alcohol levels may be determined at the request of a governing body.

B. Marijuana

Marijuana is not prohibited. However, tests may be carried out at the request of a governing body.

C. Local anaesthetics

Injectable local anaesthetics are permitted under the following conditions:
a) that *procaine, xylocaine, carbocaine, etc.* are used but **not cocaine**;
b) only *local or intra-articular injections* may be administered;
c) only when *medically justified* (ie. the details including diagnosis, dose and route of administration must be submitted immediately in writing to the IOC Medical Commission).

D. Corticosteroids

The naturally occurring and synthetic corticosteroids are mainly used as anti-inflammatory drugs which also relieve pain. They influence circulating concentrations of natural corticosteroids in the body. They produce euphoria and side effects such that their medical use, except when used topically, requires medical control.

Since 1975, the IOC Medical Commission has attempted to restrict their use during competition by requiring a declaration by doctors, because it was known that corticosteroids were being used non-therapeutically by the oral, rectal, intramuscular and even the intravenous route in some sports. However, the problem was not solved by these restrictions and therefore stronger measures designed not to interfere with the appropriate medical use of these compounds became necessary.

The use of corticosteroids is banned except for topical use (aural, ophthalmological and dermatological), inhalational therapy (asthma, allergic rhinitis) and local or intra-articular injections.

Note. Any team doctor wishing to administer corticosteroids intra-articularly or locally to a competitor must give written notification to the IOC Medical Commission.

Reproduced with modifications, with the kind permission of the Medical Commission of the International Olympic Committee.

Note. As a guide topical rectal corticosteroids are included in the banned list if the systemic blood levels of corticosteroids achieved via rectal administration are comparable to levels achieved after oral ingestion.

SUPPLEMENTARY NOTES

Caffeine

The IOC Medical Commission has banned the use of large amounts of caffeine. A urinary concentration of 12 microgram/mL must be exceeded before a sample is considered positive. However, the social use of caffeine prior to competition, eg. a cup of coffee, cola drink, bar of chocolate, should not produce a positive result unless excessive amounts are consumed.

Herbal preparations

Some herbal preparations may contain banned substances from naturally occurring plants. If taken, they may bring about a positive finding of a banned substance. Presently, there is no requirement for a comprehensive listing of ingredients in nutritional supplements. It is advisable to avoid products containing the natural occurring plant Ma Huang (chinese ephedra) as this plant contains the stimulant substance ephedrine. Commercial ginseng preparations may also contain substitute or additional substances.

Drug control policy

Different sporting organisations may ban different drugs, therefore drug control policy of the relevant governing body should be well known. Prior to an event check with the relevant governing body.

Further information is available from:

Doping Control Unit
The Sports Council
Walkden House
3-10 Melton Street
London NW1 2EB
Tel: 071-383 5667
071-383 5411

A Guide to Drugs & Sport

Drugs & Sport is presented in two sections:

1. Banned Products, Substances, Methods - Pink Pages

2. Permitted Products - Green Pages

---

1. Banned Products, Substances, Methods

Alphabetical listing including proprietary products, generic/brand cross references, other substances and methods.

a. Banned Products
Proprietary products:
  eg. **Aspav** — Brand name
  (Aspirin, **papaveretum**) — Generic component(s) - **(banned component in bold)**
  Roussel — Manufacturer

b. Banned Substances — Generic references:
Proprietary products:
  eg. **Codeine**   1B   Refer to Brand(s): Codis,.......

c. Banned Methods
  eg. *Blood Doping*

Each entry in the Pink Pages may have any or all of the following:

IOC Category: Refer to Explanations of Doping Classes and Methods

Indications: Any symptom, sign or circumstance that points to a specific treatment for an illness.

Contraindications: Any fact or circumstance that renders a particular course of treatment inadvisable or undesirable.

Adverse Reactions: An (usually) undesirable result of drug or other form of therapy in addition to the desired therapeutic effect. Whether they occur is dependent on the individual and the dose.

Comments: Additional relevant information that may assist in the clarification of why a substance is abused/banned, or cautionary notes.

2. Permitted Products

Listed alphabetically by Brand name within therapeutic classes.

The Manufacturer appears in brackets immediately after the product name.

This list is not exhaustive, nor should it be taken as a recommendation of the relevant efficacy of the various substances.

PoM preceding the Brand name indicates that the product is available on prescription only.

Cautionary Notes

— Different sporting organisations may ban different drugs. Before an event check with the relevant governing body.

— Banned substances are not only contained in medicines which may be prescribed by doctors. They can be found in over the counter preparations which can be purchased without a prescription at a pharmacy or supermarket.

— New pharmaceuticals are continually being produced; therefore no list of banned or permitted drugs is ever absolutely complete.

— Do not use medicines from overseas unless they are cleared by the governing body medical officer.

— Lists of banned drugs are periodically revised. Always check with the medical officer about medicines well before competition.

— Drug control policy of the relevant international sporting organisation or governing body should be well known. Medical officers must liaise closely with their governing body.

— Some medicines have similar brand names. One may contain a banned drug, the other may not, eg.
    Benylin Chesty Cough does not contain a banned drug
    Benylin Mentholated contains a banned stimulant.

— Do not rely on brand names of medicines that can be purchased overseas. A permitted brand name in the United Kingdom may contain a banned substance in its overseas version.

— The family doctor or local pharmacist may not be fully aware of the drug restrictions at sporting events. Always check medicines with the governing body medical officer.

— Some so-called 'vitamin' preparations and nutritional supplements may contain banned drugs eg.
    Villescon contains a banned stimulant.

— Beware 'vitamin' preparations that can be purchased overseas.

— Particular attention should be given to medicines containing combinations of drugs.

IF THERE ARE ANY DOUBTS AFTER CONSULTING DRUGS & SPORT

DOCTORS: DON'T GIVE IT

COMPETITORS: DON'T TAKE IT

Banned Products,
Substances, Methods

Brand (Generic) Manufacturer	IOC Category	Indications	Contraindications
Acebutolol	1D		Refer to Brand(s): Secadrex, Sectral
Acetazolamide	1E		Refer to Brand(s): Diamox
Acezide (Hydrochlorothiazide, captopril) Duncan Flockhart & Co	1E	Mild to moderate hypertension in patients stabilised on individual components (same proportion)	Concomitant lithium; anuria; porphyria; pregnancy, lactation
Actifed (Pseudoephedrine, triprolidine) Wellcome	1A	Upper respiratory tract congestion incl. sinuses, antra and eustachian tubes in the common cold, hayfever, allergic rhinitis, vasomotor rhinitis	MAOIs (concomitant or within 14 days); severe hypertension; severe coronary heart disease
Actifed Compound Linctus (Pseudoephedrine, dextromethorphan, triprolidine) Wellcome	1A	Unproductive cough relief, upper respiratory tract congestion ± allergic component	MAOIs (concomitant or within 14 days); severe hypertension, coronary artery disease; asthma cough; excessive accompanying secretions
Actifed Expectorant (Pseudoephedrine, guaiphenesin, triprolidine) Wellcome	1A	Decongestant cough suppressant, expectorant (and antihistamine)	MAOIs (concomitant or within 14 days); severe hypertension; severe coronary heart disease
Adrenaline	1A		Refer to Brand(s): Brovon, Epifrin, Eppy, Ganda, Isopto Epinal, Marcain with Adrenaline, Medihaler Epi, Min-I-Jet Adrenaline, Min-I-Jet Lignocaine HCl with Adrenaline, Simplene, Xylocaine with Adrenaline
Alcohol	*3A*		
Aldactide 50 (Spironolactone, hydroflumethazide) Gold Cross	1E	Congestive cardiac failure	Anuria; acute renal insufficiency, impairment; hyperkalaemia, hypercalcaemia; Addison's disease; hypersensitivity; concurrent potassium sparing diuretics, potassium supplements
Aldactone (Spironolactone) Searle	1E	Aldosterone antagonist (potassium sparing). congestive heart failure; hepatic cirrhosis with ascites and oedema; malignant ascites; nephrotic syndrome; diagnosis and treatment of primary aldosteronism	Acute or significant renal insufficiency, anuria, hyperkalaemia; Addison's disease; hypersensitivity; concurrent potassium sparing diuretics, potassium supplements; pregnancy
Alfentanil			Refer to Brand(s): Rapifen

THE DOPING DEFINITION OF THE IOC MEDICAL COMMISSION IS BASED ON THE BANNING OF PHARMACEUTICAL CLASSES OF AGENTS.

Adverse Reactions	Comments
Hypotension; fluid, electrolyte disturbances; skin reactions; dry cough; others, consult literature	Deliberate attempts to reduce weight artificially in order to compete in lower weight classes or to dilute urine constitute clear manipulations which are unacceptable on ethical grounds
Drowsiness; insomnia; urinary retention in males with prostatic enlargement	
Drowsiness; insomnia; decreased alertness; urinary retention in males with prostatic enlargement	
Drowsiness; insomnia; urinary retention in males with prostatic enlargement	
	Subject to certain restrictions, refer to Explanations of Doping Classes and Methods
Breast enlargement (usually reversible); GI intolerance; drowsiness, lethargy, headache, mental confusion, ataxia; skin reactions; endocrine disturbances; fluid, electrolyte imbalance; haematological disturbances; orthostatic hypotension; consult literature	Deliberate attempts to reduce weight artificially in order to compete in lower weight classes or to dilute urine constitute clear manipulations which are unacceptable on ethical grounds
Breast enlargement (usually reversible); fluid/electrolyte disturbances; gastrointestinal symptoms incl. cramping and diarrhoea; drowsiness; lethargy; headache; mental confusion, ataxia; skin reactions; endocrine disturbances	Deliberate attempts to reduce weight artificially in order to compete in lower weight classes or to dilute urine constitute clear manipulations which are unacceptable on ethical grounds

ANY RELATED COMPOUND TO THE EXAMPLES LISTED ABOVE ARE ALSO BANNED.

Brand (Generic) Manufacturer	IOC Category	Indications	Contraindications
Aller-eze Plus (Clemastine, phenylpropanol-amine) *Intercare*	1A	Nasal and sinus congestion; allergy, hayfever	
Alupent Tablets and Syrup (Orciprenaline) *Boehringer Ingelheim*	1A	Relief of bronchospasm in asthma, bronchitis and emphysema	Thyrotoxicosis
Aluzine (Frusemide) *Steinhard*	1E	Loop diuretic. Oedema; mild or moderate hypertension	Anuria; electrolyte deficiency; hepatic precoma
Amilco (Amiloride, hydro-chlorothiazide) *Norton*	1E	Potassium sparing diuretic. Hypertension; congestive heart failure; hepatic cirrhosis with ascites	Hyperkalaemia; concomitant potassium supplements or potassium sparing drugs/diuretics; anuria, acute renal failure; severe progressive renal disease; severe hepatic failure; hepatic precoma; Addison's disease; hypercalcaemia; concurrent lithium; diabetic nephropathy; hyperuricaemia; diabetes mellitus
Amiloride	1E		Refer to Brand(s): Amilco, Amiloride (Wyeth), Amilospare, Berkamil, Burinex A, Co-Amilozide, Frumil, Hypertane, Kalten, Lasoride, Midamor, Moducren, Moduret 25, Moduretic, Navispare, Normetic, Vasetic
Amiloride (Wyeth) (Amiloride) *Wyeth*	1E	Potassium sparing diuretic. Hypertension; congestive heart failure; hepatic cirrhosis with ascites	Hyperkalaemia; concomitant potassium supplements or potassium sparing drugs/diuretics; anuria; acute renal failure; severe progressive renal disease; diabetic nephropathy; children

THE DOPING DEFINITION OF THE IOC MEDICAL COMMISSION IS BASED ON THE BANNING OF PHARMACEUTICAL CLASSES OF AGENTS.

Adverse Reactions	Comments
Sympathomimetic side effects such as: tremor; palpitation; tachycardia; headache; nausea, abdominal discomfort	Orciprenaline via inhalation is permitted; oral forms are banned
Nausea; malaise; gastrointestinal upset; electrolyte, fluid disturbances; headache; hypotension; muscle cramps	Deliberate attempts to reduce weight artificially in order to compete in lower weight classes or to dilute urine constitute clear manipulations which are unacceptable on ethical grounds
Anorexia, nausea, vomiting, abdominal fullness, gastric irritation, cramping, pain, constipation, diarrhoea; dry mouth and thirst; paraesthesias; transient blurred vision; inflammation of a salivary gland; dizziness, vertigo, weakness, fatigability; muscle cramps; orthostatic hypotension; skin rash, pruritus; minor psychiatric disturbances; transient visual disturbances; haematological disturbances; purpura; rash; vasculitis; fever; respiratory distress; headache; restlessness; jaundice; pancreatitis; xanthopsia; hyperglycaemia; glycosuria; hyperuricaemia	Deliberate attempts to reduce weight artificially in order to compete in lower weight classes or to dilute urine constitute clear manipulations which are unacceptable on ethical grounds
Hyperkalaemia; nausea; anorexia; abdominal pain; flatulence; mild skin rash; headache; weakness; fatigability; back pain; chest pain; neck/shoulder ache; pain in extremities; angina pectoris; orthostatic hypotension; arrhythmia; palpitation; vomiting, diarrhoea, constipation; gastrointestinal bleeding; jaundice; thirst; dyspepsia, heartburn, flatulence; dry mouth; alopecia; muscle cramps; joint pain; dizziness, vertigo; paraesthesia; tremors; encephalopathy; nervousness, mental confusion, insomnia; decreased libido; depression; somnolence; cough, dyspnoea; nasal congestion; visual disturbances, increased intraocular pressure; tinnitus; impotence; polyuria, dysuria, bladder spasms, frequency of micturition	Deliberate attempts to reduce weight artificially in order to compete in lower weight classes or to dilute urine constitute clear manipulations which are unacceptable on ethical grounds

ANY RELATED COMPOUND TO THE EXAMPLES LISTED ABOVE ARE ALSO BANNED.

Brand (Generic) Manufacturer	IOC Category	Indications	Contraindications
Amilospare (Amiloride) *Ashbourne*	1E	Potassium sparing diuretic. Hypertension; congestive heart failure; hepatic cirrhosis with ascites	Hyperkalaemia; concomitant potassium supplements or potassium sparing drugs/ diuretics; anuria; acute renal failure; severe progressive renal disease; diabetic nephropathy; children
Anapolon 50 (Oxymetholone) *Syntex*	1C	Treatment of aplastic and refractory anaemias	Carcinoma of breast or prostrate in male patients; frank hepatic dysfunction, nephrosis, breast carcinoma in women with hypercalcaemia; nephrosis, pregnancy, lactation; infants; hypersensitivity
Angilol (Propranolol) *DDSA*	1D	Nonselective β-blocker. Hypertension, angina pectoris, cardiac arrhythmias (eg. anxiety tachycardia), essential tremor, phaeochromocytoma, hypertrophic subaortic stenosis; prophylaxis of migraine and recurrent vascular headaches; suspected or definite myocardial infarction	2nd or 3rd degree heart block; cardiogenic shock; bronchospasm; prolonged fasting; metabolic acidosis
Anodesyn (Ephedrine, lignocaine, allantoin) *Crookes*	1A	Haemorrhoids	Anorectal infections
Antipressan (Atenolol) *Berk*	1D	Hypertension; angina pectoris; cardiac dysrhythmias; use during acute phase following myocardial infarction	Patients with 2nd or 3rd degree heart block; pregnancy
Antoin (Codeine, *caffeine*, aspirin) *Cox*	1B	Compound analgesic. Moderate pain, antipyretic	Gastrointestinal tract disturbances

THE DOPING DEFINITION OF THE IOC MEDICAL COMMISSION IS BASED ON THE BANNING OF PHARMACEUTICAL CLASSES OF AGENTS.

Adverse Reactions	Comments
Hyperkalaemia; nausea; anorexia; abdominal pain; flatulence; mild skin rash; headache; weakness; fatigability; back pain; chest pain; neck/shoulder ache; pain in extremities; angina pectoris; orthostatic hypotension; arrhythmia; palpitation; vomiting, diarrhoea, constipation; gastrointestinal bleeding; jaundice; thirst; dyspepsia, heartburn, flatulence; dry mouth; alopecia; muscle cramps; joint pain; dizziness, vertigo; paraesthesia; tremors; encephalopathy; nervousness, mental confusion, insomnia; decreased libido; depression; somnolence; cough, dyspnoea; nasal congestion; visual disturbances, increased intraocular pressure; tinnitus; impotence; polyuria, dysuria, bladder spasms, frequency of micturition	Deliberate attempts to reduce weight artificially in order to compete in lower weight classes or to dilute urine constitute clear manipulations which are unacceptable on ethical grounds
Psychological changes incl. euphoria, depression, psychosis; salt and water retention; gynaecomastia, testicular atrophy, decreased spermatogenesis; changes in libido, prostatic hypertrophy, decreased FSH and LH level; acne, alopecia; tendon ruptures; increased LDL cholesterol, decreased HDL cholesterol; hypertension, atherogenesis, sudden death; kidney tumours; increased transaminases, cholestatic jaundice, peliosis hepatitis; hepatoma, carcinoma of the liver Additionally in females: virilising effects, menstrual disturbances, infertility In children: premature epiphyseal closure; premature virilisation	Misused in sport, not only to attempt to increase muscle bulk, strength and power when used with increased food intake but also in lower doses and normal food intake to attempt to improve competitiveness
Hypotension; bradycardia; cold extremities; headache; sleep disturbances; angina; dry eyes; skin rash	Misuse in some sports where physical activity is of little or no importance; the IOC Medical Commission reserves the right to test those sports which it deems are appropriate
Allergic skin reactions	
Bradycardia; coldness of extremities; muscle fatigue; sleep disturbances (rare); skin rashes, dry eyes	Misuse in some sports where physical activity is of little or no importance; the IOC Medical Commission reserves the right to test those sports which it deems are appropriate
Gastrointestinal bleeding; constipation, nausea, vomiting; dizziness, drowsiness	

ANY RELATED COMPOUND TO THE EXAMPLES LISTED ABOVE ARE ALSO BANNED.

Brand (Generic) Manufacturer	IOC Category	Indications	Contraindications
Apisate (**Diethylpropion**, B group vitamins) *Wyeth*	1A	Anorectic; adjunct to treatment of moderate to severe obesity	Emotionally unstable individuals; MAOIs (concomitant or within 14 days); advanced arteriosclerosis; hyperthyroidism; severe hypertension; glaucoma; other appetite suppressant drugs; pregnancy
Aprinox (**Bendrofluazide**) *Boots*	1E	Thiazide diuretic. Oedema of cardiac, renal or hepatic origin; hypertension; lactation suppression	Severe renal failure; pregnancy, lactation
Apsolol (**Propranolol**) *APS*	1D	Nonselective β-blocker. Hypertension, angina pectoris, cardiac arrhythmias (eg. anxiety tachycardia), essential tremor, phaeochromocytoma, hypertrophic subaortic stenosis; prophylaxis of migraine and recurrent vascular headaches; suspected or definite myocardial infarction	2nd or 3rd degree heart block; cardiogenic shock; bronchospasm; prolonged fasting; metabolic acidosis
Apsolox (**Oxprenolol**) *APS*	1D	Angina pectoris; hypertension; cardiac arrhythmias; short-term relief of somatic symptoms of anxiety; other cardiovascular indications, consult literature	2nd or 3rd degree heart block; marked bradycardia; uncontrolled heart failure; cardiogenic shock; sick-sinus syndrome; bronchial asthma; anaesthesia with ether, chloroform
Aramine (**Metaraminol**) *Merck Sharp & Dohme*	1A	Prevention and treatment of acute hypotension	Cyclopropane or halothane anaesthesia
Arelix (**Piretanide**) *Hoechst*	1E	Diuretic. Mild to moderate hypertension	Severe electrolyte imbalance; hypovolaemia; hypotension
Asmaven Tablets (**Salbutamol**) *APS*	1A	Bronchial asthma, conditions associated with reversible airways obstruction; bronchospasm in patients with co-existing heart disease or hypertension; management of premature labour	Diabetes mellitus; serious cardiovascular disorders, hypertension; concomitant β-blockers
Aspav (**Aspirin, papaveretum**) *Roussel*	1B	Analgesic. Relief of moderate to severe pain in post-operative states; relief of chronic pain associated with inoperable carcinoma	Respiratory depression; obstructive airways disease; MAOIs (concomitant or within 14 days)
Atenolol	1D		Refer to Brand(s): Antipressan, Atenix, Atenolol, Beta-adalat, Kalten, Tenif, Tenoret 50, Tenoretic, Tenormin, Vasaten

THE DOPING DEFINITION OF THE IOC MEDICAL COMMISSION IS BASED ON THE BANNING OF PHARMACEUTICAL CLASSES OF AGENTS.

Adverse Reactions	Comments
Dependence; headache; allergic and other rashes	
Potassium depletion; fluid and electrolyte disturbances; gastrointestinal symptoms; occasional skin rash; blood dyscrasias (rarely)	Deliberate attempts to reduce weight artificially in order to compete in lower weight classes or to dilute urine constitute clear manipulations which are unacceptable on ethical grounds
Hypotension; bradycardia; cold extremities; headache; sleep disturbances; angina; dry eyes; skin rash	Misuse in some sports where physical activity is of little or no importance; the IOC Medical Commission reserves the right to test those sports which it deems are appropriate
Hypotension; bradycardia; cold extremities; headache; sleep disturbances; dizziness, drowsiness; insomnia; excitement; dry mouth; vision disturbances; keratoconjunctivitis; loss of libido; gastrointestinal disturbances; bronchospasm; dyspnoea; heart failure	Misuse in some sports where physical activity is of little or no importance; the IOC Medical Commission reserves the right to test those sports which it deems are appropriate
Rapidly induced hypertensive responses; ventricular extrasystoles; sinus or ventricular tachycardia; consult literature	
Gastrointestinal upset; allergic reactions; fluid, electrolyte disturbances	Deliberate attempts to reduce weight artificially in order to compete in lower weight classes or to dilute urine constitute clear manipulations which are unacceptable on ethical grounds
Fine tremor of skeletal muscle	Salbutamol via inhalation only is permitted; oral and injectable forms are banned
Tolerance, dependence; nausea, vomiting, constipation; confusion	Pain of the severity to necessitate narcotic analgesia (with the risk of drug dependence), should prevent sports participation

ANY RELATED COMPOUND TO THE EXAMPLES LISTED ABOVE ARE ALSO BANNED.

Brand (Generic) Manufacturer	IOC Category	Indications	Contraindications
Atenolol **(Atenolol)** *APS* *Cox* *Evans* *Kerfoot*	1D	Cardioselective β_1-blocker. Hypertension; angina pectoris; cardiac dysrhythmias; early intervention in the acute phase of myocardial infarction	2nd or 3rd degree heart block; cardiogenic shock
Atenix **(Atenolol)** *Ashbourne*	1D	Cardioselective β_1-blocker. Hypertension; angina pectoris; cardiac dysrhythmias; early intervention in the acute phase of myocardial infarction	2nd or 3rd degree heart block; cardiogenic shock
Baycaron **(Mefruside)** *Bayer*	1E	Diuretic. Hypertension, oedema	Severe renal failure; hepatic coma; Addison's disease; severe hypercalcaemia; concurrent lithium therapy; pregnancy, lactation
Bedranol SR **(Propranolol)** *Lagap*	1D	Nonselective β-blocker. Hypertension, angina pectoris, cardiac arrhythmias (eg. anxiety tachycardia), essential tremor, phaeochromocytoma, hypertrophic subaortic stenosis; prophylaxis of migraine and recurrent vascular headaches; suspected or definite myocardial infarction	2nd or 3rd degree heart block; cardiogenic shock; bronchospasm; prolonged fasting; metabolic acidosis
Beecham's **Powders Capsules** (Paracetamol, **phenylephrine,** *caffeine)* *SmithKline Beecham*	1A	Colds and flu; decongestion; catarrh	
Bendrofluazide	1E		Refer to Brand(s): Aprinox, Berkozide, Centyl, Centyl-K, Corgaretic, Inderetic, Inderex, Neo-Naclex, Neo-Naclex-K, Prestim
Benemid **(Probenecid)** *Merck Sharp & Dohme*	2B	Hyperuricaemia in gout and gouty arthritis except presenting acute attack; to increase and prolong plasma levels in penicillin and cephalosporin therapy	Acute gouty attack; concomitant use with aspirin; blood dyscrasias; uric acid kidney stones; children <2 years
Benylin Day & **Night (Daytime tablets)** (Paracetamol, **phenylpropanol-** **amine)** *Warner-Lambert*	1A	Colds and flu	

THE DOPING DEFINITION OF THE IOC MEDICAL COMMISSION IS BASED ON THE BANNING OF PHARMACEUTICAL CLASSES OF AGENTS.

Adverse Reactions	Comments
Hypotension; bradycardia; cold extremities; headache; muscular fatigue; sleep disturbances; skin rash; dry eyes	Misuse in some sports where physical activity is of little or no importance; the IOC Medical Commission reserves the right to test those sports which it deems are appropriate
Hypotension; bradycardia; cold extremities; headache; muscular fatigue; sleep disturbances; skin rash; dry eyes	Misuse in some sports where physical activity is of little or no importance; the IOC Medical Commission reserves the right to test those sports which it deems are appropriate
Initial dyspepsia, nausea; hypokalaemia; impotence (high dosage)	Deliberate attempts to reduce weight artificially in order to compete in lower weight classes or to dilute urine constitute clear manipulations which are unacceptable on ethical grounds
Hypotension; bradycardia; cold extremities; headache; sleep disturbances; angina; dry eyes; skin rash	Misuse in some sports where physical activity is of little or no importance; the IOC Medical Commission reserves the right to test those sports which it deems are appropriate
Headache; gastrointestinal upset; urinary frequency; hypersensitivity reactions; sore gums; flushing; dizziness; anaemia; exacerbation of gout	Substances and methods which alter the integrity of urine samples used in doping controls are banned

ANY RELATED COMPOUND TO THE EXAMPLES LISTED ABOVE ARE ALSO BANNED.

Brand (Generic) Manufacturer	IOC Category	Indications	Contraindications
Benylin Mentholated (Menthol, dextromethorphan, diphenhydramine, **pseudoephedrine**) *Warner-Lambert*	1A	Cough (colds)	Cardiovascular disorders; hyperthyroidism; MAOIs (concomitant or within 14 days)
Benylin with Codeine (**Codeine**, diphenhydramine, sodium citrate, menthol) *Warner-Lambert*	1B	Cough: dry, unproductive, irritating	Hepatic disease
Benzthiazide	1E		Refer to Brand(s): Dytide
Berkamil (Amiloride) *Berk*	1E	Potassium sparing diuretic. Hypertension; congestive heart failure; hepatic cirrhosis with ascites	Hyperkalaemia; concomitant potassium supplements or potassium sparing drugs / diuretics; anuria; acute renal failure; severe progressive renal disease; diabetic nephropathy; children
Berkolol (Propranolol) *Berk*	1D	Nonselective β-blocker. Hypertension, angina pectoris, cardiac arrhythmias (eg. anxiety tachycardia), essential tremor, phaeochromocytoma, hypertrophic subaortic stenosis; prophylaxis of migraine and recurrent vascular headaches; suspected or definite myocardial infarction	2nd or 3rd degree heart block; cardiogenic shock; bronchospasm; prolonged fasting; metabolic acidosis
Berkozide (Bendrofluazide) *Berk*	1E	Oedema, hypertension	Hypercalcaemia; renal failure; Addison's disease; porphyria
Berotec Aerosol, Respirator Solution (Fenoterol) *Boehringer Ingelheim*	1A	Treatment of reversible airways obstruction as in bronchial asthma, bronchitis and emphysema	

THE DOPING DEFINITION OF THE IOC MEDICAL COMMISSION IS BASED ON THE BANNING OF PHARMACEUTICAL CLASSES OF AGENTS.

Adverse Reactions	Comments
Drowsiness	
Constipation	Cough and cold preparations which contain drugs of the narcotic analgesic class are banned
Hyperkalaemia; nausea; anorexia; abdominal pain; flatulence; mild skin rash; headache; weakness; fatigability; back pain; chest pain; neck/shoulder ache; pain in extremities; angina pectoris; orthostatic hypotension; arrhythmia; palpitation; vomiting, diarrhoea, constipation; gastrointestinal bleeding; jaundice; thirst; dyspepsia, heartburn, flatulence; dry mouth; alopecia; muscle cramps; joint pain; dizziness, vertigo; paraesthesia; tremors; encephalopathy; nervousness, mental confusion, insomnia; decreased libido; depression; somnolence; cough, dyspnoea; nasal congestion; visual disturbances, increased intraocular pressure; tinnitus; impotence; polyuria, dysuria, bladder spasms, frequency of micturition	Deliberate attempts to reduce weight artificially in order to compete in lower weight classes or to dilute urine constitute clear manipulations which are unacceptable on ethical grounds
Hypotension; bradycardia; cold extremities; headache; sleep disturbances; angina; dry eyes; skin rash	Misuse in some sports where physical activity is of little or no importance; the IOC Medical Commission reserves the right to test those sports which it deems are appropriate
Gout; skin rash, photosensitivity; thrombocytopenia; impotence (reversible)	Deliberate attempts to reduce weight artificially in order to compete in lower weight classes or to dilute urine constitute clear manipulations which are unacceptable on ethical grounds
Tachycardia; palpitation; tremor	It is an effective β_2 agonist but is banned even in aerosol form because it is metabolised to p-hydroxyamphetamine

ANY RELATED COMPOUND TO THE EXAMPLES LISTED ABOVE ARE ALSO BANNED.

Brand (Generic) Manufacturer	IOC Category	Indications	Contraindications
Beta-Adalat (Atenolol, nifedipine) *Bayer*	1D	Hypertension, angina pectoris (where therapy with either a calcium channel blocker or β-blocker proves inadequate)	Cardiogenic shock; overt heart failure; pregnancy, lactation; other cardio-depressants
Beta-Cardone (Sotalol) *Duncan Flockhart*	1D	Angina pectoris; hypertension; cardiac arrhythmias; thyrotoxicosis	Heart block; history of bronchospasm; pregnancy, lactation
Betadren (Pindolol) *Lagap*	1D	Hypertension; angina pectoris	Cardiac failure (unless controlled); heart block; pronounced bradycardia; obstructive pulmonary disease; cor pulmonale; metabolic acidosis; prolonged fasting; severe renal failure; concomitant calcium channel blockers; pregnancy, lactation
Betagan (Levobunolol) *Allergan*	1D	Reduction of intraocular pressure in chronic open-angle glaucoma and ocular hypertension	Bronchial asthma; chronic obstructive pulmonary disease; sinus bradycardia; 2nd and 3rd degree atrioventricular block; cardiac failure; cardiogenic shock
Betaloc (Metoprolol) *Astra*	1D	Cardioselective β_1-blocker Hypertension; angina pectoris; adjunct in hyperthyroidism; suspected or definite myocardial infarction; migraine prophylaxis Intravenously: disturbances of cardiac rhythm, in particular supraventricular tachyarrhythmias	Atrioventricular block; uncontrolled heart failure; severe bradycardia; sick sinus syndrome; cardiogenic shock
Betamethasone	3D		Refer to Brand(s): Betnelan, Betnesol
Betaxolol	1D		Refer to Brand(s): Betoptic
Betim (Timolol) *Leo*	1D	Angina pectoris due to ischaemic heart disease; hypertension; myocardial re-infarction; migraine prophylaxis	Heart failure (unless adequately controlled); sinus bradycardia, heart block; cardiogenic shock; bronchial asthma; chronic obstructive pulmonary disease; concomitant MAOIs; anaesthesia with agents producing myocardial depression; pregnancy
Betnelan (Betamethasone) *Glaxo*	3D	Corticosteroid responsive conditions	Systemic infections (unless specifically treated); live virus immunisation
Betnesol Tablets, Injection (Betamethasone) *Glaxo*	3D		Refer: Betnelan

THE DOPING DEFINITION OF THE IOC MEDICAL COMMISSION IS BASED ON THE BANNING OF PHARMACEUTICAL CLASSES OF AGENTS.

Adverse Reactions	Comments
Headache; flushing; fatigue; dizziness; oedema; skin rashes; dry eyes	Misuse in some sports where physical activity is of little or no importance; the IOC Medical Commission reserves the right to test those sports which it deems are appropriate
Skin rashes; dry eyes; tachycardia	Misuse in some sports where physical activity is of little or no importance; the IOC Medical Commission reserves the right to test those sports which it deems are appropriate
Depression; diarrhoea; insomnia; headaches; sleep disturbances; epigastric pain; fatigue; dizziness; hypotension; consult literature	Misuse in some sports where physical activity is of little or no importance; the IOC Medical Commission reserves the right to test those sports which it deems are appropriate
Transient burning, stinging on instillation; local ocular reactions; bradycardia; hypotension; dyspnoea, asthma; skin reactions	
Lassitude; gastrointestinal disturbances; sleep pattern disturbance; hypotension; bradycardia; cold extremities; headache; angina	Misuse in some sports where physical activity is of little or no importance; the IOC Medical Commission reserves the right to test those sports which it deems are appropriate
Gastrointestinal upset; dizziness; insomnia; sedation; depression; weakness; dyspnoea; bradycardia; heart block; bronchospasm; heart failure; skin rash; dry eyes	Misuse in some sports where physical activity is of little or no importance; the IOC Medical Commission reserves the right to test those sports which it deems are appropriate
Mask infection; fluid, electrolyte disturbances; growth retardation in infancy, childhood, adolescence; subcapsular cataracts; skin thinning; cataracts; glaucoma; aseptic osteo-necrosis; peptic ulcer	Oral corticosteroids are banned

ANY RELATED COMPOUND TO THE EXAMPLES LISTED ABOVE ARE ALSO BANNED.

Brand (Generic) Manufacturer	IOC Category	Indications	Contraindications
Betnovate Rectal (Betamethasone, **phenylephrine,** lignocaine) *Glaxo*	1A	External haemorrhoids; relief of itching, discomfort, pain assoc. with local noninfective anal, perianal conditions	Primary cutaneous viral infections
Betoptic **(Betaxolol)** *Alcon*	1D	Reduction of elevated intraocular pressure; chronic open angle glaucoma, ocular hypertension	Sinus bradycardia (>1st degree block); cardiogenic shock; history overt cardiac failure
Bisopropol	1D		Refer to Brand(s): Emcor, Monocor
Blocadren **(Timolol)** *Merck Sharp & Dohme*	1D	Nonselective β-blocker. Angina pectoris due to ischaemic heart disease; essential hypertension; long-term prevention of myocardial infarction; migraine prophylaxis	Bronchospasm; chronic obstructive pulmonary disease; allergic rhinitis; sinus bradycardia; A-V block; overt heart failure; congestive heart failure; right ventricular failure secondary to pulmonary hypertension; significant cardiomegaly; cardiogenic shock
Blood Doping	2A		
Bricanyl Tablets, **Syrup, Injection** **(Terbutaline)** *Astra*	1A	Relief of bronchospasm in bronchopulmonary conditions	Any condition of mother or fetus in which prolongation of pregnancy is hazardous
Bronalin Dry **Cough Elixir** **(Pseudoephedrine,** dextromethorphan) *Cupal*	1A	Dry coughs	
Bronchilator **(Phenylephrine,** **isoetharine)** *Sterling Winthrop*	1A	Relief of bronchospasm in bronchial asthma and chronic bronchitis	Concomitant MAOIs
Bronchodil **(Reproterol)** *Degussa*	1D	Bronchial asthma; acute, chronic bronchitis; emphysema	
Brovon **(Adrenaline,** atropine, papaverine) *Torbet*	1A	Compound bronchodilator	

THE DOPING DEFINITION OF THE IOC MEDICAL COMMISSION IS BASED ON THE BANNING OF PHARMACEUTICAL CLASSES OF AGENTS.

Adverse Reactions	Comments
Systemic corticosteroid effects, local atrophic skin changes	
Local reactions including tearing	Misuse in some sports where physical activity is of little or no importance; the IOC Medical Commission reserves the right to test those sports which it deems are appropriate
Hypotension; bradycardia; cold extremities; headache; dreams; angina	Misuse in some sports where physical activity is of little or no importance; the IOC Medical Commission reserves the right to test those sports which it deems are appropriate
Development of allergic reactions (rash, fever, etc.), acute haemolytic reaction with kidney damage if incorrectly typed blood is used, delayed transfusion reactions, transmission of infectious diseases, overload of the circulation	*These procedures contravene the ethics of medicine and sport*
Tremor; tonic cramp; palpitations; other less common reactions	Terbutaline via inhalation only is permitted; oral and injectable forms are banned
Tachycardia; palpitations; headache; blood pressure changes	
Digital tremor; palpitations; tachycardia; restlessness	
Anxiety; tremor; tachycardia, arrhythmias; dry mouth, cold extremities	

ANY RELATED COMPOUND TO THE EXAMPLES LISTED ABOVE ARE ALSO BANNED.

Brand (Generic) Manufacturer	IOC Category	Indications	Contraindications
Bumetanide	1E		Refer to Brand(s): Burinex, Burinex A, Burinex K
Buprenorphine	1B		Refer to Brand(s): Temgesic
Burinex (Bumetanide) *Leo*	1E	Loop diuretic. Oedema	Anuria; hepatic coma; severe electrolyte depletion; concomitant lithium
Burinex A (Bumetanide, amiloride) *Leo*	1E	Diuresis	Hyperkalaemia; severe electrolyte imbalance; renal insufficiency; severe renal, hepatic disease; hepatic precoma; adrenocortical insufficiency
Burinex K (Bumetanide, potassium) *Leo*	1E	As for Burinex; also potassium supplementation	Concurrent potassium sparing diuretics, potassium supplements
Cabdrivers (Phenylephrine, ephedrine) *De Witt*	1A	Colds	
Caffeine	1A		
CAM (Ephedrine) *Rybar*	1A	Bronchospasm in children and adults with asthma or bronchitis; unproductive cough	Severe heart disease; hypertension; thyrotoxicosis; concomitant MAOIs, sympathomimetics
Canreonate potassium	1E		Refer to Brand(s): Spiroctan-M
Capozide (Hydrochloro-thiazide, captopril) *Princeton*	1E	Mild to moderate hypertension in patients stabilised on individual components (same proportions)	Anuria; pregnancy, lactation
Cardinol (Propranolol) *CP Pharmaceuticals*	1D	Hypertension; angina pectoris; long-term prophylaxis of myocardial reinfarction; cardiac dysrhythmias; migraine prophylaxis; essential tremor; anxiety tachycardia; adjunct in thyrotoxicosis; phaeochromo-cytoma	2nd or 3rd degree atrioventricular block; bronchospasm; metabolic acidosis; severe bradycardia; heart failure; hypotension; intermittent claudication; pregnancy
Cartelol	1D		Refer to Brand(s): Cartrol, Teoptic

THE DOPING DEFINITION OF THE IOC MEDICAL COMMISSION IS BASED ON THE BANNING OF PHARMACEUTICAL CLASSES OF AGENTS.

Adverse Reactions	Comments
Abdominal pain; vomiting; dyspepsia; diarrhoea; stomach muscle cramps; dizziness; headache; nausea; hypotension; fluid and electrolyte imbalance	Deliberate attempts to reduce weight artificially in order to compete in lower weight classes or to dilute urine constitute clear manipulations which are unacceptable on ethical grounds
Muscle cramps; GI upset; fluid electrolyte imbalance	Deliberate attempts to reduce weight artificially in order to compete in lower weight classes or to dilute urine constitute clear manipulations which are unacceptable on ethical grounds
Refer Burinex	
	The definition of a positive result is: if the concentration of caffeine in urine >12 microgram/mL *Refer to Explanations of Doping Classes and Methods, Supplementary Notes*
Blood dyscrasias; fluid, electrolyte disturbances; hypotension; skin reactions	Deliberate attempts to reduce weight artificially in order to compete in lower weight classes or to dilute urine constitute clear manipulations which are unacceptable on ethical grounds
Gastrointestinal disturbances; fatigue; depression; dizziness; confusion; sleep disturbances; hallucinations; flushing; skin rashes; dry mouth; fluid retention; pulmonary oedema; weight gain; muscle cramps; other, consult literature	Misuse in some sports where physical activity is of little or no importance; the IOC Medical Commission reserves the right to test those sports which it deems are appropriate

ANY RELATED COMPOUND TO THE EXAMPLES LISTED ABOVE ARE ALSO BANNED.

Brand (Generic) Manufacturer	IOC Category	Indications	Contraindications
Cartrol (Cartelol) *Sanofi*	1D	Nonselective β-blocker. Angina pectoris	Severe bradycardia; 2nd or 3rd degree A-V block; cardiogenic shock; uncontrolled heart failure; metabolic acidosis; severe renal failure
Catarrh-Ex (Paracetamol, pseudoephedrine) *Thompson Medical*	1A	Congestion associated with pain and fever	
Catheterisation	2B		
Centyl (Bendrofluazide) *Leo*	1E	Hypertension, oedema	Anuria; severe renal or hepatic failure; hypercalcaemia; concurrent lithium
Centyl-K (Bendrofluazide, potassium) *Leo*	1E	As for Centyl; potassium conservation	As for Centyl; concomitant potassium supplements, potassium sparing drugs/ diuretics
Chlorothiazide	1E		Refer to Brand(s): Saluric
Chlorthalidone	1E		Refer to Brand(s): Hygroton, Hygroton K, Kalspare, Lopresoretic, Tenoret 50, Tenoretic
Chorionic gonadotrophin	1F		Refer to Brand(s): Gonadotraphon L.H., Pregnyl, Profasi
Clopamide	1E		Refer to Brand(s): Viskaldix
Co-amilofruse	1E		Refer to Brand(s): Frumil, Lasoride
Co-amilozide	1E		Refer to Brand(s): Amilco, Co-Amilozide (Lagap), Hypertane, Moduret 25, Moduretic, Normetic
Co-Amilozide (Amiloride, hydro-chlorothiazide) *Lagap*	1E	Potassium sparing diuretic. Hypertension; congestive heart failure; hepatic cirrhosis with ascites	Hyperkalaemia; concomitant potassium supplements or potassium sparing drugs/ diuretics; anuria, acute renal failure, severe progressive renal disease; severe hepatic failure; hepatic precoma; Addison's disease; hypercalcaemia; concurrent lithium; diabetic nephropathy; hyperuricaemia; diabetes mellitus

THE DOPING DEFINITION OF THE IOC MEDICAL COMMISSION IS BASED ON THE BANNING OF PHARMACEUTICAL CLASSES OF AGENTS.

Adverse Reactions	Comments
Nausea; lassitude; dizziness; hypotension; bradycardia; pain in extremities; headache; diarrhoea	Misuse in some sports where physical activity is of little or no importance; the IOC Medical Commission reserves the right to test those sports which it deems are appropriate
	Substances and methods which alter the integrity of urine samples used in doping controls are banned
Impotence; fluid, electrolyte disturbances; muscle pain, fatigue; gastrointestinal upset; oliguria; skin rash	Deliberate attempts to reduce weight artificially in order to compete in lower weight classes or to dilute urine constitute clear manipulations which are unacceptable on ethical grounds
As for Centyl	Deliberate attempts to reduce weight artificially in order to compete in lower weight classes or to dilute urine constitute clear manipulations which are unacceptable on ethical grounds
Anorexia, nausea, vomiting, abdominal fullness, gastric irritation, cramping, pain, constipation, diarrhoea; dry mouth and thirst; paraesthesias; transient blurred vision; inflammation of a salivary gland; dizziness, vertigo, weakness, fatigability; muscle cramps; orthostatic hypotension; skin rash, pruritus; minor psychiatric disturbances; transient visual disturbances; haematological disturbances; purpura; rash; vasculitis; fever; respiratory distress; headache; restlessness; jaundice; pancreatitis; xanthopsia; hyperglycaemia; glycosuria; hyperuricaemia	Deliberate attempts to reduce weight artificially in order to compete in lower weight classes or to dilute urine constitute clear manipulations which are unacceptable on ethical grounds

ANY RELATED COMPOUND TO THE EXAMPLES LISTED ABOVE ARE ALSO BANNED.

Brand (Generic) Manufacturer	IOC Category	Indications	Contraindications
Co-Betaloc, Co-Betaloc SA (Metoprolol, hydro-chlorothiazide) Astra	1D, 1E	Management of mild or moderate hypertension	Uncontrolled heart failure; severe bradycardia; sick-sinus syndrome; cardiogenic shock; severe peripheral arterial disease; severe hepatic, renal failure; therapy resistant hypokalaemia and hyponatraemia; hypercalcaemia, symptomatic hyperuricaemia, anuria; concomitant lithium
Cocaine	1A, 3C	*Surface anaesthetic, ear, nose and throat surgery*	
Co-codamol	1A		Refer to Brand(s): Panadeine Co, Paracodol
Co-codaprin	1A		Refer to Brand(s): Codis
Coda-Med (Paracetamol, *caffeine*, codeine) Broad Laboratories	1B	Tension headache (symptomatic relief)	
Codanin (Paracetamol, codeine) Whitehall	1B	Moderate pain and fever	
Codeine	1B		Refer to Brand(s): Antoin, Benylin, (Co-codamol), (Co-codaprin), Coda-Med, Codanin, Codis, Cojene, Diarrest, Dimotane Co, Dimotane Co Paediatric, Feminax, Flurex Bedtime Cold Remedy, Flurex Hot Lemon Concentrate, Formulix, Galcodine, Hypon, Jacksons Night Cough Pastilles, Kaodene, Medocodene, Migraleve, Migralift, Panadeine Co, Panerel, Paracodol, Parahypon, Paradale, Parake, Phensedyl, Propain, Pulmo Baily, Solpadeine, Solpadol, Syndol, Tercoda, Terpoin, Tylex, Uniflu, Veganin
Codis (Aspirin, codeine) Reckitt & Colman	1B	Relief of moderate pain; anti-inflammatory, antipyretic	Gastrointestinal tract disturbances
Co-dydramol			Refer to Brand(s): Galake, Paramol
Cojene (Aspirin, codeine, *caffeine)* Fisons	1B	Relief of moderate pain; anti-inflammatory, antipyretic	Gastrointestinal tract disturbances

THE DOPING DEFINITION OF THE IOC MEDICAL COMMISSION IS BASED ON THE BANNING OF PHARMACEUTICAL CLASSES OF AGENTS.

Adverse Reactions	Comments
Lassitude; gastrointestinal disturbances; sleep disturbances; metabolic and electrolyte disturbances; others, consult literature	Deliberate attempts to reduce weight artificially in order to compete in lower weight classes or to dilute urine constitute clear manipulations which are unacceptable on ethical grounds Misuse in some sports where physical activity is of little or no importance; the IOC Medical Commission reserves the right to test those sports which it deems are appropriate
Dependence, abuse	*Stimulants increase alertness, reduce fatigue, may increase competitiveness and hostility*
Dependence, tolerance; nausea, vomiting, constipation; dizziness, drowsiness	
Gastrointestinal bleeding; constipation, nausea, vomiting; dizziness, drowsiness; see product literature	
Gastrointestinal bleeding; constipation; nausea, vomiting; dizziness, drowsiness	

ANY RELATED COMPOUND TO THE EXAMPLES LISTED ABOVE ARE ALSO BANNED.

Brand (Generic) Manufacturer	IOC Category	Indications	Contraindications
Coldrex Powders (Paracetamol, **phenylephrine,** vitamin C) *Sterling Health*	1A	Colds and flu	
Coldrex Tablets (Paracetamol, **pseudoephedrine,** *caffeine,* terpin, vitamin C) *Sterling Health*	1A	Colds and flu	
Colifoam Rectal Foam (Hydrocortisone) *Stafford Miller*	3D	Topical treatment of inflammation of rectal mucosa	Obstruction; abscess; perforation; peritonitis; fresh intestinal anastamoses; extensive fistulas; fungal, viral infection
Collis Browne's Mixture (Anhydrous morphine, peppermint oil) *International*	1B	Diarrhoea; stomach upset	Children <6 years
Collis Browne's Tablets (Morphine, kaolin, calcium carbonate) *International*	1B	Diarrhoea in colic; mild gastroenteritis	
Congesteze (Azantadine, **pseudoephedrine)** *Schering-Plough*	1A	Relief of symptoms of upper respiratory mucosal congestion in allergic rhinitis	Concurrent MAOIs; cardiac asthma
Co-proxamol	1B		Refer to Brand(s): Cosalgesic, Distalgesic, Paxalgesic
Contac 400 (Phenylpropanol- amine, chlor- pheniramine) *SmithKline Beecham*	1A	Colds	
Corgard (Nadolol) *Squibb*	1D	Angina pectoris, cardiac arrhythmias, hypertension; migraine prophylaxis; thyrotoxicosis (adjunct)	Bronchospasm; right ventricular failure secondary to pulmonary hypertension; sinus bradycardia; 2nd & 3rd degree A-V block; cardiogenic shock; congestive heart failure

THE DOPING DEFINITION OF THE IOC MEDICAL COMMISSION IS BASED ON THE BANNING OF PHARMACEUTICAL CLASSES OF AGENTS.

Adverse Reactions	Comments
Systemic effects of corticosteroids possible; consult literature	Topical rectal administration of corticosteroids is banned because the systemic blood levels of corticosteroids achieved via rectal administration are comparable to levels after oral ingestion
Drowsiness; epigastric distress; weakness; nervousness	
Drowsiness; gastrointestinal upset	
Gastrointestinal upset; hypotension; bradycardia; cold extremities; headache; depression; insomnia; mouth dryness; alopecia	Misuse in some sports where physical activity is of little or no importance; the IOC Medical Commission reserves the right to test those sports which it deems are appropriate

ANY RELATED COMPOUND TO THE EXAMPLES LISTED ABOVE ARE ALSO BANNED.

Brand (Generic) Manufacturer	IOC Category	Indications	Contraindications
Corgaretic (Nadolol, bendrofluazide) *Squibb*	1D, 1E	Hypertension	Bronchial asthma; sinus bradycardia; 2nd & 3rd degree heart block; cardiogenic shock; right ventricular failure secondary to pulmonary hypertension; congestive heart failure; anuria
Cortisone	3D		Refer to Brand(s): Cortison Acetate MSD, Cortistab, Cortisyl
Cortisone Acetate MSD (Cortisone) *MSD*	3D	Corticosteroid responsive conditions	Tuberculosis; diabetes; osteoporosis; hypertension; severe affective disorders; glaucoma; previous steroid myopathy; peptic ulceration; epilepsy; live virus immunisation
Cortistab (Cortisone) *Boots*	3D	Corticosteroid responsive conditions, eg. Addison's disease; primary or secondary adrenal insufficiency; congenital adrenal hyperplasia	Tuberculosis; diabetes; osteoporosis; hypertension; severe affective disorders; glaucoma; previous steroid myopathy; peptic ulceration; epilepsy; live virus immunisation
Cortisyl (Cortisone) *Roussel*	3D	Corticosteroid responsive conditions, eg. Addison's disease; primary or secondary adrenal insufficiency; congenital adrenal hyperplasia	Tuberculosis; diabetes; osteoporosis; hypertension; severe affective disorders; glaucoma; previous steroid myopathy; peptic ulceration; epilepsy; live virus immunisation
Corwin (Xamoterol) *Stuart*	1A	Chronic mild to moderate heart failure	Severe heart failure; lactation
Cosalgesic (Dextropropoxyphene, paracetamol) *Cox*	1B	Management of mild to moderate pain	Alcohol; suicidal or emotionally unstable individuals
Cyclimorph (Morphine) *Wellcome*	1B	Relief of severe pain with associated nausea	Respiratory depression; obstructive airways disease; MAOIs (concomitant or within 14 days)
Cyclopenthiazide	1E		Refer to Brand(s): Navidrex, Navidrex-K, Navispare, Trasidrex

THE DOPING DEFINITION OF THE IOC MEDICAL COMMISSION IS BASED ON THE BANNING OF PHARMACEUTICAL CLASSES OF AGENTS.

Adverse Reactions	Comments
Gastrointestinal upset; bradycardia; fatigue; light headedness; cold extremities; depression; insomnia; paraesthesia; mouth dryness; alopecia; hypotension	Misuse in some sports where physical activity is of little or no importance; the IOC Medical Commission reserves the right to test those sports which it deems are appropriate Deliberate attempts to reduce weight artificially in order to compete in lower weight classes or to dilute urine constitute clear manipulations which are unacceptable on ethical grounds
Gastrointestinal upset incl. peptic ulcer; osteoporosis and long bone fractures; fluid and electrolyte disturbances; impaired skin healing; thin fragile skin; decreased carbohydrate tolerance; muscle weakness, myopathy, aseptic necrosis, tendon rupture, osteoporosis; cataract, increased intraocular and intracranial pressure; psychic derangements; hypothalamic pituitary adrenal axis suppression	Oral corticosteroids are banned
Gastrointestinal upset incl. peptic ulcer; osteoporosis and long bone fractures; fluid and electrolyte disturbances; impaired skin healing; thin fragile skin; decreased carbohydrate tolerance; muscle weakness, myopathy, aseptic necrosis, tendon rupture, osteoporosis; cataract, increased intraocular and intracranial pressure; psychic derangements; hypothalamic pituitary adrenal axis suppression	Oral corticosteroids are banned
Gastrointestinal upset incl. peptic ulcer; osteoporosis and long bone fractures; fluid and electrolyte disturbances; impaired skin healing; thin fragile skin; decreased carbohydrate tolerance; muscle weakness, myopathy, aseptic necrosis, tendon rupture, osteoporosis; cataract, increased intraocular and intracranial pressure; psychic derangements; hypothalamic pituitary adrenal axis suppression	Oral corticosteroids are banned
Gastrointestinal disturbances; headache, dizziness; chest pain; palpitations; muscle cramp; skin rash	
Dependence; dizziness; sedation; nausea, vomiting, constipation, abdominal pain; skin rash; lightheadedness; headache; weakness; euphoria, dysphonia, visual disturbances	Pain of the severity to necessitate narcotic analgesia (with the risk of drug dependence), should prevent sports participation
Tolerance, dependence; drowsiness; dry mouth; blurred vision	Pain of the severity to necessitate narcotic analgesia (with the risk of drug dependence), should prevent sports participation

ANY RELATED COMPOUND TO THE EXAMPLES LISTED ABOVE ARE ALSO BANNED.

Brand (Generic) Manufacturer	IOC Category	Indications	Contraindications
Daranide **(Dichlorphenamide)** *Merck Sharp &* *Dohme*	1E	Chronic simple (open angle) glaucoma; secondary glaucoma; pre-op control of intraocular tension in acute angle glaucoma	Hepatic insufficiency; renal failure; adrenocortical insufficiency; hyperchloraemic acidosis; depressed sodium or potassium levels; chronic noncongestive closed angle glaucoma; severe pulmonary obstruction; pregnancy
Davenol **(Ephedrine,** carbinoxamine, pholcoline) *Whitehall*	1A	Cough	Cardiovascular disorders; hyperthyroidism; hepatic disease; MAOIs (concomitant or within 14 days)
Day Nurse **Capsules, Liquid** (Paracetamol, dextromethorphan, **phenylpropanol-** **amine)** *SmithKline* *Beecham*	1A	Cold remedy (day time)	
Deca-Durabolin **(Nandrolone)** *Organon*	1C	Osteoporosis in post-menopausal women	Prostatic carcinoma, breast carcinoma in male; pregnancy, lactation
Deca-Durabolin **100** **(Nandrolone)** *Organon*	1C	Blood disorders incl: anaemia of chronic renal failure; aplastic anaemia; anaemia due to cytotoxic disease	Refer: Deca-Durabolin
Decadron **(Dexamethasone)** *Merck Sharpe &* *Dohme*	3D	Corticosteroid responsive conditions incl. cerebral oedema; diagnostic testing of adrenocortical hyperfunction	Systemic fungal infection
Decadron Injection **(Dexamethasone)** *Merck Sharpe &* *Dohme*	3D	Corticosteroid responsive conditions	Systemic fungal infection

THE DOPING DEFINITION OF THE IOC MEDICAL COMMISSION IS BASED ON THE BANNING OF PHARMACEUTICAL CLASSES OF AGENTS.

Adverse Reactions	Comments
Gastrointestinal disturbances (anorexia, nausea and vomiting), loss of weight, constipation; urinary frequency, renal colic, renal calculi; skin eruptions, pruritus; blood dyscrasias; headache; weakness; nervousness; globus hystericus; sedation, lassitude, depression, confusion, disorientation, dizziness, ataxia, tremor; tinnitus; paraesthesiae of the hands, feet, tongue	Deliberate attempts to reduce weight artificially in order to compete in lower weight classes or to dilute urine constitute clear manipulations which are unacceptable on ethical grounds
Drowsiness; constipation; tachycardia; arrhythmias; dry mouth; CNS stimulation	Cough and cold preparations which contain drugs of the narcotic analgesic and stimulant classes are banned
Psychological changes incl. euphoria, depression, psychosis; salt and water retention; gynaecomastia, testicular atrophy, decreased spermatogenesis; changes in libido, prostatic hypertrophy, decreased FSH and LH level; acne, alopecia; tendon ruptures; increased LDL cholesterol, decreased HDL cholesterol; hypertension, atherogenesis, sudden death; kidney tumours; increased transaminases, cholestatic jaundice, peliosis hepatitis; hepatoma, carcinoma of the liver Additionally in females: virilising effects, menstrual disturbances, infertility In children: premature epiphyseal closure; premature virilisation	Misused in sport not only to attempt to increase muscle bulk, strength and power when used with increased food intake but also in lower doses and normal food intake to attempt to improve competitiveness
Refer: Deca-Durabolin	Refer: Deca-Durabolin
Sodium and fluid retention; peptic ulcer with possible perforation; muscle weakness and myopathy; osteoporosis; tendon rupture; aseptic necrosis; impaired wound healing, thin fragile skin; growth suppression; decreased carbohydrate tolerance; psychic derangements; increased intraocular and intracranial pressure; cataracts; hypothalamic pituitary adrenal axis suppression	Oral corticosteroids are banned
Sodium, fluid retention; peptic ulcer with possible perforation; impaired wound healing, thin fragile skin; decreased carbohydrate tolerance; growth suppression; muscle weakness, myopathy, aseptic necrosis, tendon rupture, osteoporosis; cataract, increased intraocular and intracranial pressure; psychic derangements; hypothalamic pituitary adrenal axis suppression	Parenteral corticosteroids are banned

ANY RELATED COMPOUND TO THE EXAMPLES LISTED ABOVE ARE ALSO BANNED.

Brand (Generic) Manufacturer	IOC Category	Indications	Contraindications
Decadron Phosphate Shock Pak (Dexamethasone) *Merck Sharp & Dohme*	3D	Adjunctive therapy in treatment of shock	Systemic fungal infections; sulphite sensitivity
Decortisyl (Prednisone) *Roussel*	3D	Corticosteroid responsive states	Systemic fungal infections; peptic ulcer; osteoporosis
Deltacortril (Prednisolone) *Pfizer*	3D	Steroid responsive disorders	Systemic fungal infections unless specific anti-infective therapy employed
Deltastab (Prednisolone) *Boots*	3D	Corticosteroid responsive states	Systemic fungal infections; peptic ulcer; osteoporosis
Depo-Medrone (Methyl-prednisolone) *Upjohn*	3D	Corticosteroid responsive conditions	Systemic fungal infection; concomitant immunisation; intravenous, intrathecal administration
Dexamethasone	3D		Refer to Brand(s): Decadron, Decadron Injection, Decadron Shock Pak, Oradexon
Dexamphetamine	1A		Refer to Brand(s): Dexedrine
Dexedrine (Dexamphetamine) *Evans*	1A	Hyperkinetic behaviour disorders in children; narcolepsy	MAOIs (concomitant or within 14 days); cardiovascular disease; moderate to severe hypertension; hyperthyroidism; hyperexcitability; glaucoma
Dextromoramide	1B		Refer to Brand(s): Palfium
Dextropropoxy-phene	1B		Refer to Brand(s): (Co-proxamol), Cosalgesic, Distalgesic, Doloxene, Doloxene Co., Paxalgesic
DF 118 (Dihydrocodeine) *Duncan Flockhart*	1B	Moderate to severe pain; antitussive	Respiratory depression; obstructive airways disease; asthma attacks

THE DOPING DEFINITION OF THE IOC MEDICAL COMMISSION IS BASED ON THE BANNING OF PHARMACEUTICAL CLASSES OF AGENTS.

Adverse Reactions	Comments
Sodium, fluid retention; peptic ulcer with possible perforation; impaired wound healing, thin fragile skin; decreased carbohydrate tolerance; growth suppression; muscle weakness, myopathy, aseptic necrosis, tendon rupture, osteoporosis; cataract, increased intraocular and intracranial pressure; psychic derangements; hypothalamic pituitary adrenal axis suppression	Parenteral corticosteroids are banned
Sodium, fluid retention; peptic ulcer with possible perforation; impaired wound healing, thin fragile skin; decreased carbohydrate tolerance; growth suppression; muscle weakness, myopathy, aseptic necrosis, tendon rupture, osteoporosis; cataract, increased intraocular and intracranial pressure; psychic derangements; hypothalamic pituitary adrenal axis suppression	Oral corticosteroids are banned
Sodium, fluid retention; peptic ulcer with possible perforation; impaired wound healing, thin fragile skin; decreased carbohydrate tolerance; growth suppression; muscle weakness, myopathy, aseptic necrosis, tendon rupture, osteoporosis; cataract, increased intraocular and intracranial pressure; psychic derangements; hypothalamic pituitary adrenal axis suppression	Oral corticosteroids are banned
Sodium, fluid retention; peptic ulcer with possible perforation; impaired wound healing, thin fragile skin; decreased carbohydrate tolerance; growth suppression; muscle weakness, myopathy, aseptic necrosis, tendon rupture, osteoporosis; cataract, increased intraocular and intracranial pressure; psychic derangements; hypothalamic pituitary adrenal axis suppression	Oral corticosteroids are banned
Salt and water retention; peptic ulcer with possible perforation; impaired wound healing, thin fragile skin; decreased carbohydrate tolerance; growth suppression; muscle weakness, myopathy, aseptic necrosis, tendon rupture, osteoporosis; cataract, increased intraocular and intracranial pressure; psychic derangements; hypothalamic pituitary adrenal axis suppression	Parenteral corticosteroids are banned
Insomnia; restlessness; irritability; euphoria; tremor; dizziness; headache; dryness of mouth; anorexia; gastrointestinal disturbances; sweating; hypertension; tachycardia; palpitation; dependence	Amphetamines have been grossly misused in sport and associated with deaths
Constipation, nausea, vomiting; headache, vertigo	Pain of the severity to necessitate narcotic analgesia should prevent sports participation. Cough and cold preparations which contain drugs of the narcotic anaglesic class are banned

ANY RELATED COMPOUND TO THE EXAMPLES LISTED ABOVE ARE ALSO BANNED.

Brand (Generic) Manufacturer	IOC Category	Indications	Contraindications
DHC Continus (Dihydrocodeine) *Napp*	1B	Relief of moderately severe pain in cancer	Respiratory depression; obstructive airways disease; asthma attacks
Diamorphine (Heroin)	1B	*Potent analgesic*	
Diamorphine Tablets (Diamorphine) *Roche*	1B	Potent analgesic	Respiratory depression; obstructive airways disease; acute alcoholism; head injury
Diamox (Acetazolamide) *Lederle*	1E	Glaucoma; oedema (incl. in congestive heart failure and drug induced); centrencephalic epilepsies	Depressed sodium and/or potassium blood levels; Addison's disease; long-term admin. in chronic noncongestive angle closure glaucoma; marked kidney or liver disease or dysfunction; adrenal gland failure, hyperchloraemic acidosis; pregnancy esp. 1st trimester
Diarrest (Codeine, dicyclomine, electrolytes) *Galen*	1B	Diarrhoea incl. electrolytes	Diarrhoea assoc. with pseudomembranous colitis; diverticular disease
Diatensec (Spironolactone) *Gold Cross*	1E	Congestive cardiac failure; hepatic cirrhosis with ascites and oedema; malignant ascites; nephrotic syndrome; diagnosis and treatment of primary aldosteronism	Anuria; renal insufficiency; hyperkalaemia; Addison's disease; concurrent potassium supplements or potassium sparing diuretics
Dichlorphenamide	1E		Refer to Brand(s): Daranide
Diconal (Dipipanone, cyclizine) *Wellcome*	1B	Analgesic with antiemetic action	Respiratory depression; obstructive airways disease; MAOIs (concomitant or within 14 days)
Diethylpropion	1A		Refer to Brand(s): Apisate, Tenuate Dospan
Dihydrocodeine	1B		Refer to Brand(s): (Co-dydramol), DF 118, DHC Continus, Parmol
Dimotane Co, Paediatric (Codeine, pseudo-ephedrine, brompheniramine) *Whitehall*	1A, 1B	Cough and congestion; hayfever	MAOIs (concomitant or within 14 days); severe hypertension, coronary heart disease

THE DOPING DEFINITION OF THE IOC MEDICAL COMMISSION IS BASED ON THE BANNING OF PHARMACEUTICAL CLASSES OF AGENTS.

Adverse Reactions	Comments
Constipation, nausea, vomiting; headache, vertigo	Pain of the severity to necessitate narcotic analgesia should prevent sports participation
Dependence, abuse	*Pain of the severity to necessitate narcotic analgesia (with the risk of drug dependence), should prevent sports participation*
Dependence, abuse; nausea, vomiting, constipation; drowsiness, confusion; respiratory depression; consult literature	Pain of the severity to necessitate narcotic analgesia (with the risk of drug dependence), should prevent sports participation
Fever; rash; crystalluria; renal calculus; bone marrow depression; haematological disturbances; paraesthesia; loss of appetite; polyuria; urticaria; melaena; haematuria; glycosuria; hepatic insufficiency; flaccid paralysis; convulsions	Deliberate attempts to reduce weight artificially in order to compete in lower weight classes or to dilute urine constitute clear manipulations which are unacceptable on ethical grounds
Nausea, vomiting; dizziness, drowsiness	
Fluid and electrolyte disturbances; breast enlargement (usually reversible); gastrointestinal intolerance; drowsiness, lethargy; headache, mental confusion; ataxia; skin rash; impotence; menstrual irregularities; mild androgenic effects	Deliberate attempts to reduce weight artificially in order to compete in lower weight classes or to dilute urine constitute clear manipulations which are unacceptable on ethical grounds
Dependence; drowsiness; mouth dryness; blurred vision; confusion	Pain of the severity to necessitate narcotic analgesia (with the risk of drug dependence), should prevent sports participation
Drowsiness; tachycardia; dry mouth; CNS stimulation; constipation	Cough and cold preparations which contain drugs of the narcotic analgesic and stimulant classes are banned

ANY RELATED COMPOUND TO THE EXAMPLES LISTED ABOVE ARE ALSO BANNED.

Brand (Generic) Manufacturer	IOC Category	Indications	Contraindications
Dimotane Plus Expectorant, Tablets (**Pseudoephedrine** , guaiphenesin, **brompheniramine**) *Whitehall*	1A	Cough	Cardiovascular disorders; hyperthyroidism
Dimotapp, Dimotapp LA (Brompheniramine, **phenylephrine, phenylpropanol- amine,** paracetamol) *Whitehall*	1A	Systemic nasal decongestant. Catarrh, allergic rhinitis, sinusitis	Cardiovascular disease; hyperthyroidism
Diocalm (**Morphine,** attapulgite) *SmithKline Beecham*	1B	Diarrhoea	
Dipivefrin	1A		Refer to Brand(s): Propine
Distalgesic (**Dextropropoxyphe- ne,** paracetamol) *Dista*	1B	Management of mild to moderate pain	Alcohol; suicidal or emotionally unstable individuals
Diumide-K Continus (**Frusemide,** potassium) *Degussa*	1E	Thiazide diuretic + potassium supplement. Oedema of cardiac, pulmonary, hepatic, renal and peripheral origin	Porphyria; hyperkalaemia; hepatic coma and precoma; Addison's disease; concomitant potassium sparing diuretics; digestive tract obstructions
Diuresal (**Frusemide**) *Lagap*	1E	Loop diuretic. Oedema; mild or moderate hypertension	Anuria; electrolyte deficiency; hepatic precoma
Diurexan (**Xipamide**) *Degussa*	1E	Hypertension; oedema	Severe electrolyte deficiency; hepatic precoma; severe renal insufficiency
Dobutamine	1A		Refer to Brand(s): Dobutrex
Dobutrex (**Dobutamine**) *Lilly*	1A	Short-term treatment in adults of cardiac failure secondary to acute myocardial infarction or cardiac surgery	

THE DOPING DEFINITION OF THE IOC MEDICAL COMMISSION IS BASED ON THE BANNING OF PHARMACEUTICAL CLASSES OF AGENTS.

Adverse Reactions	Comments
Drowsiness; tachycardia; arrhythmias; dry mouth; CNS stimulation	
Drowsiness; dry mouth	
Dependence; dizziness; sedation; nausea, vomiting, constipation, abdominal pain; skin rash; lightheadedness; headache; weakness; euphoria, dysphonia, visual disturbances	Pain of the severity to necessitate narcotic analgesia (with the risk of drug dependence), should prevent sports participation
Hyperuricaemia	Deliberate attempts to reduce weight artificially in order to compete in lower weight classes or to dilute urine constitute clear manipulations which are unacceptable on ethical grounds
Nausea; malaise; gastrointestinal upset; electrolyte, fluid disturbances; headache; hypotension; muscle cramps	Deliberate attempts to reduce weight artificially in order to compete in lower weight classes or to dilute urine constitute clear manipulations which are unacceptable on ethical grounds
Gastrointestinal disturbances; mild dizziness	Deliberate attempts to reduce weight artificially in order to compete in lower weight classes or to dilute urine constitute clear manipulations which are unacceptable on ethical grounds
Increased heart rate, blood pressure, ventricular ectopic activity; nausea; headache; anginal pain; nonspecific chest pain; palpitations; shortness of breath	

ANY RELATED COMPOUND TO THE EXAMPLES LISTED ABOVE ARE ALSO BANNED.

Brand (Generic) Manufacturer	IOC Category	Indications	Contraindications
Do-Do Tablets (Theophylline, **ephedrine, *caffeine)*** *Ciba*	1A	Bronchial cough; breathlessness, wheezing	
Doloxene, Doloxene Co (Dextropropoxy-phene, Co + aspirin, ***caffeine)*** *Lilly*	1B	Relief of mild to moderate pain	Emotionally unstable or suicidal patients
Dopacard (Dopexamine) *Fisons*	1A	Heart failure associated with cardiac surgery	MAOI therapy; left ventricular outlet obstruction; phaeochromocytoma; thrombocytopenia
Dopamine	1A		Refer to Brand(s): Dopamine HCl in 5% Dextrose Inj, Intropin, Select-A-Jet Dopamine
Dopamine Hydrochloride in 5% Dextrose Injection (Dopamine) *Abbott*	1A	Correction of poor perfusion, low cardiac output, impending renal failure and shock associated with: myocardial infarction, trauma, endotoxic septicaemia, open heart surgery, heart failure	Phaeochromocytoma; uncorrected hypovolaemia, tachyarrhythmias, ventricular fibrillation; hyperthyroidism; alkaline diluent soln
Dopram (Doxapram) *Wyeth*	1A	Ventilatory stimulant. Acute respiratory failure	Severe hypertension; status asthmaticus; coronary artery disease; thyrotoxicosis; epilepsy; physical obstruction of respiratory tract
Doxapram	1A		Refer to Brand(s): Dopram
Dristan Tablets (Phenylephrine, chlorpheniramine, aspirin, ***caffeine)*** *Whitehall*	1A	Nasal congestion, catarrh due to colds, hayfever	
Dryptal (Frusemide) *Berk*	1E	Diuretic. Oliguria management due to acute or chronic renal insufficiency	Electrolyte deficiency; hepatic cirrhosis; digitalis intoxication; advanced renal failure; prostatic hypertrophy; micturition impairment
Duovent **(Fenoterol,** ipratropium) *Boehringer Ingelheim*	1D	Treatment of reversible airways obstruction; in bronchial asthma, bronchitis, emphysema	

THE DOPING DEFINITION OF THE IOC MEDICAL COMMISSION IS BASED ON THE BANNING OF PHARMACEUTICAL CLASSES OF AGENTS.

Adverse Reactions	Comments
CNS disturbances (incl. alertness); dependence; nausea, vomiting, constipation; see product literature	Pain of the severity to necessitate narcotic analgesia (with the risk of drug dependence), should prevent sports participation
Increased heart rate; nausea, vomiting; anginal pain; tremor	
Ectopic beats; tachycardia; anginal pain; palpitations; dyspnoea; vomiting, nausea; hypotension; vasoconstriction	
Increase in blood pressure, heart rate; dizziness; consult literature	
Fluid, electrolyte imbalance; hyperuricaemia; gastrointestinal upset incl. nausea; malaise	Deliberate attempts to reduce weight artificially in order to compete in lower weight classes or to dilute urine constitute clear manipulations which are unacceptable on ethical grounds
Tachycardia; palpitation; tremor	Fenoterol is an effective β_2 agonist but is banned even in aerosol form because it is metabolised to ρ-hydroxyamphetamine

ANY RELATED COMPOUND TO THE EXAMPLES LISTED ABOVE ARE ALSO BANNED.

Brand (Generic) Manufacturer	IOC Category	Indications	Contraindications
Durabolin (Nandrolone) *Organon*	1C	Osteoporosis in post-menopausal women	Prostatic or breast carcinoma in males; pregnancy, lactation
Duromine (Phentermine) *3M Health Care*	1A	Management of moderate to severe obesity as short term adjunct to weight reduction based on calorie restriction	Severe hypertension; thyrotoxicosis; agitated states; history of drug abuse; MAOIs (concomitant or within 14 days)
Dyazide (Hydrochloro-thiazide, triamterene) *Bridge*	1E	Potassium sparing diuretic. Treatment of oedema; mild to moderate hypertension	Other potassium sparing agents; progressive renal disease; hyperkalaemia; pregnancy; lactation
Dytac (Triamterene) *Bridge*	1E	Potassium sparing diuretic. Oedema	Severe or progressive renal failure; hyperkalaemia, potassium supplements, other potassium sparing agents or potassium rich diet
Dytide (Triamterene, benzthiazide) *Bridge*	1E	Control of oedema in cardiac failure, hepatic cirrhosis, nephrotic syndrome, associated corticosteroid use	Hyperkalaemia; progressive renal failure; concomitant potassium supplements or potassium sparing drug/diuretics
Edecrin (Ethacrynic acid) *Merck Sharp & Dohme*	1E	Loop diuretic. Congestive heart failure; pulmonary and renal oedema; hepatic cirrhosis with ascites; oedema due to other causes	Anuria; infants <2 years; lactation
Efcortelan Soluble (Hydrocortisone) *Glaxo*	3D	Status asthmaticus; acute allergic reactions; anaphylactic reactions to drugs; severe shock; adrenal crisis; soft tissue conditions	Systemic infection without specific anti-infective therapy; live virus immunisation; direct injection into tendons
Efcortesol (Hydrocortisone) *Glaxo*	3D	Refer: Efcortelan	
Emcor (Bisopropol) *Merck*	1D	Hypertension; angina pectoris	Untreated cardiac failure; cardiogenic shock; sinoatrial block; 2nd or 3rd degree A-V block; marked bradycardia; extreme hypotension

THE DOPING DEFINITION OF THE IOC MEDICAL COMMISSION IS BASED ON THE BANNING OF PHARMACEUTICAL CLASSES OF AGENTS.

Adverse Reactions	Comments
Psychological changes incl. euphoria, depression, psychosis; salt and water retention; gynaecomastia, testicular atrophy, decreased spermatogenesis; changes in libido, prostatic hypertrophy, decreased FSH and LH level; acne, alopecia; tendon ruptures; increased LDL cholesterol, decreased HDL cholesterol; hypertension, atherogenesis, sudden death; kidney tumours; increased transaminases, cholestatic jaundice, peliosis hepatitis; hepatoma, carcinoma of the liver Additionally in females: virilising effects, menstrual disturbances, infertility In children: premature epiphyseal closure; premature virilisation	Misused in sport, not only to attempt to increase muscle bulk, strength and power when used with increased food intake but also in lower doses and normal food intake to attempt to improve competitiveness
CNS stimulation; vomiting; dry mouth; facial oedema; rash; headache; palpitations; tachycardia; elevation of blood pressure; psychosis; hallucinations; dependence; constipation; micturition disturbances; nausea; dizziness; nervousness; depression	
Muscle cramps; weakness; dizziness; headache; dry mouth; anaphylaxis; rash; urticaria; photosensitivity and purpura; nausea; vomiting; diarrhoea; constipation	Deliberate attempts to reduce weight artificially in order to compete in lower weight classes or to dilute urine constitute clear manipulations which are unacceptable on ethical grounds
Nausea, vomiting, diarrhoea; weakness; headache; dry mouth; minor decreases in blood pressure; anaphylaxis; photosensitivity; rash; elevated uric acid	Deliberate attempts to reduce weight artificially in order to compete in lower weight classes or to dilute urine constitute clear manipulations which are unacceptable on ethical grounds
Nausea, vomiting, diarrhoea; muscle cramps, weakness; dizziness, headache; dry mouth; decreases in blood pressure; rash; electrolyte, fluid imbalance; blood dyscrasias	Deliberate attempts to reduce weight artificially in order to compete in lower weight classes or to dilute urine constitute clear manipulations which are unacceptable on ethical grounds
Anorexia; malaise; abdominal discomfort or pain; dysphagia; nausea; vomiting and diarrhoea; reversible hyperuricaemia; decreased urinary urate excretion; hyperglycaemia; acute gout may be precipitated; haematological disturbances; deafness; tinnitus; vertigo; blurred vision; fatigue; apprehension; skin rash; headache; fever; chills; haematuria	Deliberate attempts to reduce weight artificially in order to compete in lower weight classes or to dilute urine constitute clear manipulations which are unacceptable on ethical grounds
Fluid and electrolyte retention; peptic ulcer with possible perforation; impaired wound healing, thin fragile skin; decreased carbohydrate tolerance; growth suppression; muscle weakness, myopathy, aseptic necrosis, tendon rupture, osteoporosis; cataract, increased intraocular and intracranial pressure; psychic derangements; hypothalamic pituitary adrenal axis suppression	Parenteral corticosteroids are banned
Lassitude; dizziness; mild headache; perspiration; paraesthesia of the extremities; others, consult literature	Misuse in some sports where physical activity is of little or no importance; the IOC Medical Commission reserves the right to test those sports which it deems are appropriate

ANY RELATED COMPOUND TO THE EXAMPLES LISTED ABOVE ARE ALSO BANNED.

Brand (Generic) Manufacturer	IOC Category	Indications	Contraindications
Enduron (Methyclothiazide) *Abbott*	1E	Thiazide diuretic. Mild to moderate hypertension; adjunct in resistant hypertension; oedema	Severe renal or hepatic disease; Addison's disease; hypercalcaemia; concurrent lithium
Enterosan (Morphine, kaolin, belladonna) *Windsor*	1B	Diarrhoea, colic, stomach upset	
Ephedrine	1A		Refer to Brand(s): Anodesyn, Bronalin, Cabdrivers, CAM, Davenol, Do-Do Tablets, Expurhin, Franol Expectorant, Franolyn Expectorant, Galloways, Haymine, Lotussin, Meltus, Nirolex Expectorant, Noradran, Phensedyl, Vicks Medinite, Wigglesworth
Epifrin (Adrenaline) *Allergan*	1A	Primary open angle glaucoma	Closed angle glaucoma
Epoetin alfa, beta	1F, 2B		Refer to Brand(s): Eprex, Recormon
Eppy (Adrenaline) *Smith & Nephew*	1A	Simple open angle glaucoma	Narrow angle glaucoma
Eprex (Erythropoietin) *Cilag*	1F, 2B	Correction of erythropoietin deficiency in dialysis patients with renal anaemia	
Equagesic (Ethoheptazine, meprobamate, aspirin) *Wyeth*	1B	Short-term symptomatic treatment of pain occurring in musculoskeletal disorders	Emotionally unstable patients; porphyria; peptic ulceration; haemophilia; renal disease; concurrent coumarin anticoagulants; pregnancy, lactation, children <12 years
Erythropoietin	1F, 2B		Refer to Brand(s): Eprex, Recormon
Esidrex (Hydrochloro-thiazide) *Ciba*	1E	Oedema; hypertension	Hepatic precoma; Addison's disease; advanced renal failure

THE DOPING DEFINITION OF THE IOC MEDICAL COMMISSION IS BASED ON THE BANNING OF PHARMACEUTICAL CLASSES OF AGENTS.

Adverse Reactions	Comments
Fluid and electrolyte disturbances; increases in blood urea nitrogen; serum uric acid; impotence; blood dyscrasias; consult literature	Deliberate attempts to reduce weight artificially in order to compete in lower weight classes or to dilute urine constitute clear manipulations which are unacceptable on ethical grounds
Eye discomfort; irritation and redness; headache; adrenachrome deposits in the conjunctiva and cornea	
Pain on instillation; blurred vision, photophobia, redness; pigmentary deposits in the conjunctiva; transient stinging may occur; headache; browache; palpitation; faintness; tachycardia; extrasystole; hypertension and cardiac arrhythmia	
Flu-like symptoms incl. headache, aching joints, weakness, dizziness, lassitude; blood pressure increase; increased platelet count; increased blood viscosity; shunt thromboses; hyperkalaemia	
Dependence; drowsiness; dizziness; nausea; ataxia; vomiting; hypotension; paraesthesia; paradoxical excitement; others, consult literature	Pain of the severity to necessitate narcotic analgesia (with the risk of dependence), should prevent sports participation
Fluid and electrolyte disturbances; mild anorexia, nausea, constipation, diarrhoea; skin rash; photosensitivity; blood dyscrasias (rare); decreased carbohydrate tolerance; hyperuricaemia	Deliberate attempts to reduce weight artificially in order to compete in lower weight classes or to dilute urine constitute clear manipulations which are unacceptable on ethical grounds

ANY RELATED COMPOUND TO THE EXAMPLES LISTED ABOVE ARE ALSO BANNED.

Brand (Generic) Manufacturer	IOC Category	Indications	Contraindications
Eskornade Spansule, Syrup (Diphenylpyraline, **phenylpropanol-amine**) *Smith Kline & French*	1A	Relief of respiratory tract congestion and hypersecretion assoc. with common cold; acute, chronic, allergic rhinitis; influenza; sinusitis	Hypertensive disease; severe heart disease; hyperthyroidism; glaucoma, prostatic hypertrophy; MAOI therapy (concomitant or within 14 days)
Ethacrynic Acid	1E		Refer to Brand(s): Edecrin
Ethoheptazine	1B		Refer to Brand(s): Equagesic
Exirel (Pirbuterol) *3M Health Care*	1D	Treatment and prophylaxis of bronchial asthma	Concomitant nonselectiveβ-blockers
Expulin (Chlorpheniramine, **pseudoephedrine,** pholcodine, menthol) *Galen*	1A	Cough and colds	
Expurhin (Ephedrine, chlor-pheniramine, menthol) *Galen*	1A	Paediatric linctus. Nasal decongestion	Hypertension; hyperthyroidism; coronary heart disease; diabetes; MAOIs
Famel Original (Codeine, guaiphenesin) *Crookes*	1B	Cough	
Feminax (Paracetamol, **codeine, *caffeine*)** *Nicholas*	1B	Stomach cramps, backache, headache assoc. with period pain	Glaucoma
Fenoterol	1A		Refer to Brand(s): Berotec, Duovent
Fenox (Phenylephrine) *Crookes*	1A	Nasal congestion	
Fentanyl	1B		Refer to Brand(s): Sublimaze, Thalamonal

THE DOPING DEFINITION OF THE IOC MEDICAL COMMISSION IS BASED ON THE BANNING OF PHARMACEUTICAL CLASSES OF AGENTS.

Adverse Reactions	Comments
Dry mouth; drowsiness; blurred vision; urinary hesitancy or retention; palpitations; drowsiness; insomnia	
Tremors; headache; nervousness; insomnia; palpitations	
Drowsiness	
Drowsiness	
Drowsiness	

ANY RELATED COMPOUND TO THE EXAMPLES LISTED ABOVE ARE ALSO BANNED.

Brand (Generic) Manufacturer	IOC Category	Indications	Contraindications
Florinef (Fludrocortisone) *Squibb*	3D	Partial replacement therapy for primary and secondary adrenocortical insufficiency in Addison's disease; salt-losing adrenogenital syndrome	
Fludrocortisone	3D		Refer to Brand(s): Florinef
Flurex Bedtime Cold Remedy (Paracetamol, diphenhydramine, **pseudoephedrine, codeine**) *Cupal*	1A, 1B	Flu and colds (night-time)	Asthmatics; consult physician
Flurex Capsules (Paracetamol, **phenylephrine**) *Cupal*	1A	Symptomatic relief of colds and flu	
Flurex Hot Lemon Concentrate (**Codeine, ephedrine,** diphenhydramine) *Cupal*	1A, 1B	Colds, flu and assoc. dry coughs	
Flurex Tablets (Paracetamol, **phenylephrine, *caffeine*)** *Cupal*	1A	Symptomatic relief of colds, flu and catarrh	
Formulix (**Codeine,** paracetamol) *Cilag*	1B	Relief of mild to moderate pain	
Fortagesic (**Pentazocine,** paracetamol) *Sterling Winthrop*	1B	Moderate pain in musculoskeletal conditions	Respiratory depression; raised intracranial pressure; head injuries; MAOIs (concomitant or within 14 days)
Fortral (**Pentazocine**) *Sterling Winthrop*	1B	Moderate to severe pain	Respiratory depression; raised intracranial pressure; head injuries; MAOIs (concomitant or within 14 days)

THE DOPING DEFINITION OF THE IOC MEDICAL COMMISSION IS BASED ON THE BANNING OF PHARMACEUTICAL CLASSES OF AGENTS.

Adverse Reactions	Comments
Sodium, fluid retention; muscle weakness, myopathy; aseptic necrosis, tendon rupture, osteoporosis; peptic ulcer with possible perforation; impaired wound healing, thin fragile skin; increased intracranial and intraocular pressure; growth suppression; decreased carbohydrate tolerance; cataracts; psychic derangements; hypothalamic pituitary adrenal axis suppression	Oral corticosteroids are banned
Drowsiness	Cough and cold preparations which contain drugs of the narcotic analgesic and stimulant classes are banned
Drowsiness	Cough and cold preparations which contain drugs of the narcotic analgesic and stimulant classes are banned
Lightheadedness; dizziness; sedation; nausea, vomiting	Cough and cold preparations which contain drugs of the narcotic analgesic class are banned
Dependence; sedation; dizziness; nausea	Pain of the severity to necessitate narcotic analgesia (with the risk of dependence), should prevent sports participation
Sedation; dependence; nausea; vertigo; vomiting; diaphoresis; skin flush; visual disturbances	Pain of the severity to necessitate narcotic analgesia (with the risk of drug dependence), should prevent sports participation

ANY RELATED COMPOUND TO THE EXAMPLES LISTED ABOVE ARE ALSO BANNED.

Brand (Generic) Manufacturer	IOC Category	Indications	Contraindications
Franol (**Ephedrine,** theophylline) *Sterling Winthrop*	1A	Management of bronchospasm in reversible airway obstruction assoc. with stable asthma or chronic bronchitis	Unstable angina; cardiac arrhythmias; severe hypertension; severe coronary artery disease; porphyria; pregnancy
Franol Expect (Theophylline, guaiphenesin, **ephedrine**) *Janssen*	1A	Productive cough; congested airways	
Frumax (**Frusemide**) *Ashbourne*	1E	Loop diuretic. Oedema; mild or moderate hypertension	Anuria; electrolyte deficiency; hepatic precoma
Frumil (**Frusemide, amiloride**) *Rorer*	1E	Diuretic. Congestive cardiac failure; nephrosis; corticosteroid therapy; oestrogen therapy; ascites	Hyperkalaemia; Addison's disease; acute renal failure, anuria; severe progressive renal disease; electrolyte imbalance; hepatic precoma; concomitant potassium supplements or potassium sparing drugs/ diuretics; children
Frusemide	1E		Refer to Brand(s): Aluzine, Diumide-K Continus, Diuresal, Dryptal, Frumax, Frumil, Frusemide, Frusene, Frusid, IMS Frusemide, Hydroled, Lasikal, Lasilactone, Lasipressin, Lasix Lasix + K, Lasoride
Frusene (**Frusemide, triamterene**) *Fisons*	1E	Cardiac or hepatic oedema	Severe renal or hepatic failure; hyperkalaemia; concomitant potassium supplements, or potassium sparing drugs/ diuretics
Frusid (**Frusemide**) *DDSA*	1E	Loop diuretic. Oedema; mild or moderate hypertension	Anuria; electrolyte deficiency; hepatic precoma
Galake (**Dihydrocodeine,** paracetamol) *Galen*	1B	Mild to moderate pain	Respiratory depression; chronic obstructive airways disease
Galcodine (**Codeine**) *Galen*	1B	Dry, painful cough	Hepatic disease; ventilatory failure
Galloways (**Ephedrine,** guaiphenesin) *LRC*	1A	Colds	

THE DOPING DEFINITION OF THE IOC MEDICAL COMMISSION IS BASED ON THE BANNING OF PHARMACEUTICAL CLASSES OF AGENTS.

Adverse Reactions	Comments
Arrhythmias; tachycardia; palpitation; flushing; giddiness; headache; tremor; anxiety; restlessness; insomnia; muscle weakness; nausea, vomiting, dyspepsia; thirst, sweating, difficult micturation	
Nausea; malaise; gastrointestinal upset; electrolyte, fluid disturbances; headache; hypotension; muscle cramps	Deliberate attempts to reduce weight artificially in order to compete in lower weight classes or to dilute urine constitute clear manipulations which are unacceptable on ethical grounds
Fluid and electrolyte disturbances; increased serum uric acid levels; malaise; gastric upset; nausea, vomiting, diarrhoea, constipation	Deliberate attempts to reduce weight artificially in order to compete in lower weight classes or to dilute urine constitute clear manipulations which are unacceptable on ethical grounds
Electrolyte, fluid disturbances; gastrointestinal upset; weakness, fatigue; lightheadedness or dizziness; muscle cramps; thirst; flushing; urinary frequency; skin rash	Deliberate attempts to reduce weight artificially in order to compete in lower weight classes or to dilute urine constitute clear manipulations which are unacceptable on ethical grounds
Nausea; malaise; gastrointestinal upset; electrolyte, fluid disturbances; headache; hypotension; muscle cramps	Deliberate attempts to reduce weight artificially in order to compete in lower weight classes or to dilute urine constitute clear manipulations which are unacceptable on ethical grounds
Constipation, nausea; headache, dizziness	
Constipation, respiratory depression	Cough and cold preparations which contain drugs of the narcotic analgesic class are banned

ANY RELATED COMPOUND TO THE EXAMPLES LISTED ABOVE ARE ALSO BANNED.

Brand (Generic) Manufacturer	IOC Category	Indications	Contraindications
Galpseud (Pseudoephedrine) *Galen*	1A	Nasal, sinus, upper respiratory tract congestion	Cardiovascular disorders; hyperthyroidism
Ganda (Adrenaline, guanethidine) *Smith & Nephew*	1A	Primary open angle or secondary glaucoma	Narrow angle glaucoma
Gee's Linctus (Opium)	1B		Refer to Brand(s): Gee's Linctus Pastilles, T&R Gee's Linctus, Wig Gee's
Gee's Linctus Pastilles (Opium) *Ernest Jackson*	1B	Cough	
Genotropin (Somatropin = growth hormone) *Kabivitrum*	1F	Short stature due to decreased or failed pituitary growth hormone secretion	Closed epiphyses
Gonadotraphon L.H. (Chorionic gonadotrophin) *Paines & Byrne*	1F	Anovulatory infertility (females); delayed puberty, undescended testes, oligospermia (males)	Disorders which may be exacerbated by androgen release
Gonadotrophin, chorionic	1F		Refer to Brand(s): Gonadotraphon L.H., Profasi
Growth Hormone = somatropin	1F		Refer to Brand(s): Genotropin, Humatrope, Norditropin, Saizen
Half-Inderal LA (Propranolol) *ICI*	1D		Refer: Inderal
Haymine (Ephedrine, chlorpheniramine) *Pharmax*	1A	Hayfever	
Heroin	1B		Refer to diamorphine
Humatrope (Somatropin = growth hormone) *Lilly*	1F	Treatment of growth failure in children due to deficiency of endogenous growth hormone	Closed epiphyses; active tumour

THE DOPING DEFINITION OF THE IOC MEDICAL COMMISSION IS BASED ON THE BANNING OF PHARMACEUTICAL CLASSES OF AGENTS.

Adverse Reactions	Comments
Tachycardia; arrhythmias; dry mouth, CNS stimulation	
Eye discomfort, redness; headache; irritation; local skin reactions; tachycardia; extrasystoles; increases in blood pressure	
Antibody formation; allergic reactions	Misuse of growth hormone in sport is deemed to be unethical and dangerous
Headache; tiredness; mood changes	Considered equivalent to the exogenous administration of testosterone
Antibody formation; hypothyroidism; oedema	Misuse of growth hormone in sport is deemed to be unethical and dangerous

ANY RELATED COMPOUND TO THE EXAMPLES LISTED ABOVE ARE ALSO BANNED.

Brand (Generic) Manufacturer	IOC Category	Indications	Contraindications
Hydrenox **(Hydro-flumethiazide)** *Boots*	1E	Oedema; hypertension	Severe renal failure; Addison's disease; hypercalcaemia; hepatic, renal impairment
Hydrochloro-thiazide	1E		Refer to Brand(s): Acezide, Amilco, Capozide, Co-Amilozide, Co-Betaloc, Dyazide, Esidrex, Hydromet, Hydrosaluric, Hypertane, Kalten, Moducren, Moduret 25, Moduretic, Normetic, Secadrex, Serpasil Esidrex, Sotazide, Tolerazide, Triamco, Vasetic
Hydrocortisone	3D		Refer to Brand(s): Colifoam, Efcortelan, Efcortesol, Hydrocortistab, Hydrocortone, Solu-Cortef
Hydrocortisone **Sodium Succinate** **(Hydrocortisone)** *Organon*	3D	Status asthmaticus; acute allergic reactions; anaphylactic reactions to drugs; severe shock; adrenal crisis; soft tissue conditions	Systemic infection without specific anti-infective therapy; live virus immunisation; direct injection into tendons
Hydrocortistab **Tablets** **(Hydrocortisone)** *Boots*	3D	Replacement therapy in primary, secondary or acute adrenocortical insufficiency	Systemic fungal infections
Hydrocortone **(Hydrocortisone)** *Merck Sharp & Dohme*	3D	Replacement therapy in primary, secondary or acute adrenocortical insufficiency	Systemic fungal infections
Hydro-flumethiazide	1E		Refer to Brand(s): Aldactide, Hydrenox
Hydromet **(Hydrochloro-thiazide,** methyldopa) *Merck Sharp & Dohme*	3D	Antihypertensive	Severe hepatic disease; severe renal failure, anuria; Addison's disease; hypercalcaemia; concurrent lithium; depression; phaeochromocytoma
HydroSaluric **(Hydrochloro-thiazide)** *Merck Sharp & Dohme*	1E	Thiazide diuretic. Antihypertensive	Anuria; severe renal, hepatic failure; Addison's disease; hypercalcaemia; concurrent lithium

THE DOPING DEFINITION OF THE IOC MEDICAL COMMISSION IS BASED ON THE BANNING OF PHARMACEUTICAL CLASSES OF AGENTS.

Adverse Reactions	Comments
Electrolyte, fluid imbalance; increased serum uric acid levels; decreased carbohydrate tolerance; blood dyscrasias; skin rash; impotence	Deliberate attempts to reduce weight artificially in order to compete in lower weight classes or to dilute urine constitute clear manipulations which are unacceptable on ethical grounds
Fluid and electrolyte retention; peptic ulcer with possible perforation; impaired wound healing, thin fragile skin; decreased carbohydrate tolerance; growth suppression; muscle weakness, myopathy, aseptic necrosis, tendon rupture, osteoporosis; cataract, increased intraocular and intracranial pressure; psychic derangements; hypothalamic pituitary adrenal axis suppression	Parenteral corticosteroids are banned
Fluid and electrolyte disturbances; muscle weakness; steroid myopathy; osteoporosis; aseptic necrosis; tendon rupture; peptic ulcer with possible perforation; impaired wound healing, thin fragile skin; endocrine disturbances; subcapsular cataracts; consult literature	Oral corticosteroids are banned
Fluid and electrolyte disturbances; muscle weakness; steroid myopathy; osteoporosis; aseptic necrosis; tendon rupture; peptic ulcer with possible perforation; impaired wound healing, thin fragile skin; endocrine disturbances; subcapsular cataracts; consult literature	Oral corticosteroids are banned
Sedation; headache; asthenia; depression; bradycadia; gastrointestinal upset, blood dyscrasias	Deliberate attempts to reduce weight artificially in order to compete in lower weight classes or to dilute urine constitute clear manipulations which are unacceptable on ethical grounds
Fluid and electrolyte disturbance; gastrointestinal upset; dizziness, vertigo; paraesthesia; headache; decreased carbohydrate tolerance; blood dyscrasias; hypotension; photosensitivity; rash; consult literature	Deliberate attempts to reduce weight artificially in order to compete in lower weight classes or to dilute urine constitute clear manipulations which are unacceptable on ethical grounds

ANY RELATED COMPOUND TO THE EXAMPLES LISTED ABOVE ARE ALSO BANNED.

Brand (Generic) Manufacturer	IOC Category	Indications	Contraindications
Hygroton (Chlorthalidone) Geigy	1E	Thiazide analogue diuretic. Hypertension, oedema, renal diabetes insipidus	Severe renal and hepatic failure; concomitant lithium
Hygroton K (Chlorthalidone, potassium) Geigy	1E	Refer Hygroton; potassium supplement	Refer Hygroton; in addition concomitant potassium supplements or potassium sparing drugs/diuretics
Hypertane (Hydrochloro-thiazide, amiloride) Schwarz	1E	Hypertension; congestive heart failure; hepatic cirrhosis with ascites	Hyperkalaemia; hypercalcaemia; concomitant potassium supplements or potassium sparing drugs/diuretics; severe progressive renal disease, acute renal failure; severe hepatic failure; Addison's disease; diabetic nephropathy; anuria; concurrent lithium
Hypon (Aspirin, **codeine**, **caffeine**) Wellcome	1B	Analgesic; antipyretic	Haemophiliacs; active peptic ulcer
IMS Frusemide (Frusemide) IMS	1E	Loop diuretic. Oedema; mild or moderate hypertension	Anuria; electrolyte deficiency; hepatic precoma
IMS Morphine (Morphine) IMS	1B	Severe pain	Respiratory depression; obstructive airways disease; MAOIs (concomitant or within 14 days)
Indapamide	1E		Refer to Brand(s): Natrilix
Inderal, Inderal LA (Propranolol) ICI	1D	Nonselective β-blocker. Hypertension, angina pectoris, cardiac arrhythmias (eg. anxiety tachycardia), essential tremor, phaeochromocytoma, hypertrophic subaortic stenosis; prophylaxis of migraine and recurrent vascular headaches; suspected or definite myocardial infarction	2nd or 3rd degree heart block; cardiogenic shock; bronchospasm; prolonged fasting; metabolic acidosis
Inderetic (Propranolol, bendrofluazide) ICI	1D, 1E	Hypertension	2nd or 3rd degree heart block; cardiogenic shock; bronchospasm; anuria, renal failure; prolonged fasting; metabolic acidosis

THE DOPING DEFINITION OF THE IOC MEDICAL COMMISSION IS BASED ON THE BANNING OF PHARMACEUTICAL CLASSES OF AGENTS.

Adverse Reactions	Comments
Gastrointestinal disturbances; fluid, electrolyte disturbances dizziness, tiredness; cardiac disturbances; vision disturbances; skin rash; blood dyscrasias	Deliberate attempts to reduce weight artificially in order to compete in lower weight classes or to dilute urine constitute clear manipulations which are unacceptable on ethical grounds
Refer Hygroton	Deliberate attempts to reduce weight artificially in order to compete in lower weight classes or to dilute urine constitute clear manipulations which are unacceptable on ethical grounds
Fluid, electrolyte disturbances; gastrointestinal upset; minor psychiatric disturbances; muscle cramps; dry mouth; skin rash; photosensitivity; blood dyscrasias	Deliberate attempts to reduce weight artificially in order to compete in lower weight classes or to dilute urine constitute clear manipulations which are unacceptable on ethical grounds
Gastrointestinal haemorrhage; constipation	
Nausea; malaise; gastrointestinal upset; electrolyte, fluid disturbances; headache; hypotension; muscle cramps	Deliberate attempts to reduce weight artificially in order to compete in lower weight classes or to dilute urine constitute clear manipulations which are unacceptable on ethical grounds
Tolerance, dependence; nausea, vomiting	Pain of the severity to necessitate narcotic analgesia (with the risk of drug dependence), should prevent sports participation
Hypotension; bradycardia; cold extremities; headache; sleep disturbances; angina; dry eyes; skin rash	Misuse in some sports where physical activity is of little or no importance; the IOC Medical Commission reserves the right to test those sports which it deems are appropriate
Hypotension; bradycardia; cold extremities; headache; sleep disturbances; angina; dry eyes; skin rash; gastrointestinal upset; lassitude; muscle fatigue; fluid, electrolyte disturbances; hyperuricaemia	Misuse in some sports where physical activity is of little or no importance; the IOC Medical Commission reserves the right to test those sports which it deems are appropriate Deliberate attempts to reduce weight artificially in order to compete in lower weight classes or to dilute urine constitute clear manipulations which are unacceptable on ethical grounds

ANY RELATED COMPOUND TO THE EXAMPLES LISTED ABOVE ARE ALSO BANNED.

Brand (Generic) Manufacturer	IOC Category	Indications	Contraindications
Inderex (**Propranolol, bendrofluazide**) *ICI*	1D, 1E		Refer: Inderetic
Intal Compound Spinhaler (Sodium cromoglycate, isoprenaline) *Fisons*	1A	Preventative treatment, bronchial asthma	
Intropin (**Dopamine**) *Du Pont*	1A	Correction of poor perfusion, low cardiac output, impending renal failure and shock associated with: myocardial infarction, trauma, endotoxic septicaemia, open heart surgery, heart failure	Phaeochromocytoma; uncorrected hypovolaemia, tachyarrhythmias, ventricular fibrillation; hyperthyroidism; alkaline diluent soln
Ionamin (**Phentermine**) *Lipha*	1A	Anoretic agent. Short-term adjunct in moderate to severe obesity	Severe hypertension; thyrotoxicosis; psychiatric illness; emotional instability; MAOIs (concomitant or within 14 days)
Isoetharine	1A		Refer to Brand(s): Bronchilator, Numotac
Isometheptene	1A		Refer to Brand(s): Midrid
Isoprenaline	1A		Refer to Brand(s): Intal Compound, Medihaler Iso, Min-I-Jet Isoprenaline, Saventrine
Isopto Epinal (**Adrenaline**) *Alcon*	1A	Simple open angle glaucoma	Narrow angle glaucoma
Isopto Frin (**Phenylephrine**) *Alcon*	1A	Relief of minor eye irritation in absence of infection	Contact lenses
Jackson's Night Cough Pastilles (**Codeine**, ext. wild cherry bark, benzoic acid) *Ernest Jackson*	1B	Cough	

THE DOPING DEFINITION OF THE IOC MEDICAL COMMISSION IS BASED ON THE BANNING OF PHARMACEUTICAL CLASSES OF AGENTS.

Adverse Reactions	Comments
Occasional throat, trachea irritation	
Ectopic beats; tachycardia; anginal pain; palpitations; dyspnoea; vomiting, nausea; hypotension; vasoconstriction	
Dry mouth; restlessness; nervousness; insomnia; palpitations; constipation, nausea, vomiting; skin rash; euphoria; agitation	
Extracellular pigmentation; systemic side effects incl. headaches, palpitation, pallor, tachycardia, trembling, perspiration	
Slight pupil dilation	

ANY RELATED COMPOUND TO THE EXAMPLES LISTED ABOVE ARE ALSO BANNED.

Brand (Generic) Manufacturer	IOC Category	Indications	Contraindications
Junior Mu-Cron **(Phenylpropanol-amine,** ipecacuanha) *Ciba*	1A	Catarrh, runny nose, nasal congestion	
Kalspare **(Chlorthalidone, triamterene)** *Cusi*	1E	Management of mild to moderate hypertension; oedema	Progressive renal failure; concomitant lithium; hyperkalaemia; concomitant potassium supplements or potassium sparing drugs/diuretics
Kalten **(Atenolol, hydro-chlorothiazide, amiloride)** *Stuart*	1D, 1E	Management of hypertension	2nd or 3rd degree heart block; hyperkalaemia; concomitant potassium supplements or potassium sparing drugs/diuretics; anuria, acute renal failure, severe progressive renal disease; diabetic nephropathy; elevated blood urea; cardiogenic shock
Kaodene **(Codeine,** kaolin) *Boots*	1B	Simple diarrhoea	Pseudomembranous colitis, diverticular disease
Kaolin and Morphine Mixture (Kaolin, **morphine**) *(Unbranded)*	1B	Diarrhoea	Pseudomembranous colitis, diverticular disease
Kenalog **(Triamcinolone)** *Princeton*	3D	Corticosteroid responsive conditions	
Kerlone **(Betaxolol)** *Lorex*	1D	Management of hypertension	Cardiogenic shock; uncontrolled congestive cardiac failure; 2nd or 3rd degree heart block; marked bradycardia
Labetolol	1D		Refer to Brand(s): Labetolol, Labrocol Trandate
Labetolol **(Labetolol)** *APS* *Cox* *Evans* *Kerfoot*	1D	Treatment of all grades of hypertension; angina pectoris with existing hypertension; IV: rapid control of blood pressure, hypertensive episodes following acute myocardial infarction	2nd or 3rd degree heart block; cardiogenic shock; other conditions assoc. with severe and prolonged hypotension or severe bradycardia

THE DOPING DEFINITION OF THE IOC MEDICAL COMMISSION IS BASED ON THE BANNING OF PHARMACEUTICAL CLASSES OF AGENTS.

Adverse Reactions	Comments
Hyperuricaemia; fluid or electrolyte disturbances; nausea, dry mouth, constipation; leg cramp; headaches; dizziness, fatigue	
Cold extremities; muscular fatigue; bradycardia; sleep disturbances; skin rash; dry eyes; gastrointestinal upset; dry mouth; thirst; paraesthesia; blurred vision; vertigo; fatigue; hypotension; dizziness; headache; skin rash; photosensitivity; blood dyscrasias; consult literature	Deliberate attempts to reduce weight artificially in order to compete in lower weight classes or to dilute urine constitute clear manipulations which are unacceptable on ethical grounds Misuse in some sports where physical activity is of little or no importance; the IOC Medical Commission reserves the right to test those sports which it deems are appropriate
Large doses: drowsiness, CNS depression	
Large doses: drowsiness, CNS depression	
Dyspepsia; peptic ulcer with perforation, haemorrhage; osteoporosis; vertebral and long bone fractures; tendon rupture; sodium, water retention; thin fragile skin, impaired wound healing; growth suppression; impaired carbohydrate tolerance; endocrine disturbances; others, consult literature	Parenteral corticosteroids are banned
Lassitude; cold extremities; bradycardia; A-V block; cardiac insufficiency; bronchospasm; rash; dry eyes	Misuse in some sports where physical activity is of little or no importance; the IOC Medical Commission reserves the right to test those sports which it deems are appropriate
Hypotension; bradycardia; cold extremities; headache; tiredness; depression; dizziness; lethargy; nasal congestion; sweating; tremor; difficult micturition; epigastric pain; nausea, vomiting; consult literature	Misuse in some sports where physical activity is of little or no importance; the IOC Medical Commission reserves the right to test those sports which it deems are appropriate

ANY RELATED COMPOUND TO THE EXAMPLES LISTED ABOVE ARE ALSO BANNED.

Brand (Generic) Manufacturer	IOC Category	Indications	Contraindications
Labrocol (**Labetolol**) *Lagap*	1D		Refer: Labetolol
Laractone (**Spironolactone**) *Lagap*	1E	Aldosterone antagonist (potassium sparing). congestive heart failure; hepatic cirrhosis with ascites and oedema; malignant ascites; nephrotic syndrome; diagnosis and treatment of primary aldosteronism	Acute or significant renal insufficiency, anuria, hyperkalaemia; Addison's disease; hypersensitivity; concurrent potassium sparing diuretics, potassium supplements; pregnancy
Lasikal (**Frusemide,** potassium) *Hoechst*	1E	Treatment of oedema where potassium supplementation required	As for Lasix; plus concomitant potassium supplements or potassium sparing drugs/ diuretics
Lasilactone (**Frusemide, spironolactone**) *Hoechst*	1E	Resistant oedema associated with secondary hyperaldosteronism	Renal insufficiency; anuria; hyperkalaemia; Addison's disease; concomitant potassium supplements or potassium sparing drugs/ diuretics
Lasipressin (**Frusemide, penbutolol**) *Hoechst*	1D, 1E	Management of mild to moderate hypertension	Severe bradycardia; conduction defects; cardiogenic shock; metabolic acidosis; bronchial asthma; chronic obstructive airways disease; allergic rhinitis; peripheral circulatory disorders; concurrent myocardial depressant anaesthetics; anuria; hepatic coma; hypokalaemia; hypovolaemia; hyponatraemia; end stage renal failure; phaeochromocytoma
Lasix (**Frusemide**) *Hoechst*	1E	Loop diuretic. Oedema; mild or moderate hypertension	Anuria; electrolyte deficiency; hepatic precoma
Lasix K (**Frusemide,** potassium) *Hoechst*	1E	As for Lasix; plus potassium conservation	As for Lasix; plus concomitant potassium supplements, potassium sparing drugs/ diuretics
Lasoride (**Frusemide, amiloride**) *Hoechst*	1E	Diuresis where potassium conservation is important	Hyperkalaemia; Addison's disease; acute renal failure, anuria, severe progressive renal disease; electrolyte imbalance; hepatic precoma; concomitant potassium supplements or potassium sparing drugs/ diuretics
Ledercort (**Triamcinolone**) *Lederle*	3D	Corticosteroid responsive conditions	Tuberculosis, Herpes simplex; active peptic ulcer; acute glomerulonephritis; myasthenia gravis; osteoporosis; fresh intestinal anastomoses; diverticulitis; thrombo- phlebitis; psychic disturbances; pregnancy; local or systemic infections

THE DOPING DEFINITION OF THE IOC MEDICAL COMMISSION IS BASED ON THE BANNING OF PHARMACEUTICAL CLASSES OF AGENTS.

Adverse Reactions	Comments
Breast enlargement (usually reversible); fluid/electrolyte disturbances; gastrointestinal symptoms incl. cramping and diarrhoea; drowsiness; lethargy; headache; mental confusion, ataxia; skin reactions; endocrine disturbances	Deliberate attempts to reduce weight artificially in order to compete in lower weight classes or to dilute urine constitute clear manipulations which are unacceptable on ethical grounds
As for Lasix	Deliberate attempts to reduce weight artificially in order to compete in lower weight classes or to dilute urine constitute clear manipulations which are unacceptable on ethical grounds
Fluid, electrolyte disturbances; muscle weakness, cramps; gastrointestinal upset; headache; hypotension; drowsiness; breast enlargement (usually reversible); endocrine changes; consult literature	Deliberate attempts to reduce weight artificially in order to compete in lower weight classes or to dilute urine constitute clear manipulations which are unacceptable on ethical grounds
As for Lasix; also CNS disturbances; gastrointestinal upset; bronchospasm	Misuse in some sports where physical activity is of little or no importance; the IOC Medical Commission reserves the right to test those sports which it deems are appropriate Deliberate attempts to reduce weight artificially in order to compete in lower weight classes or to dilute urine constitute clear manipulations which are unacceptable on ethical grounds
Nausea; malaise; gastrointestinal upset; electrolyte, fluid disturbances; headache; hypotension; muscle cramps	Deliberate attempts to reduce weight artificially in order to compete in lower weight classes or to dilute urine constitute clear manipulations which are unacceptable on ethical grounds
As for Lasix	Deliberate attempts to reduce weight artificially in order to compete in lower weight classes or to dilute urine constitute clear manipulations which are unacceptable on ethical grounds
Electrolyte, fluid disturbances; malaise; gastric upset; skin rash; others, consult literature	Deliberate attempts to reduce weight artificially in order to compete in lower weight classes or to dilute urine constitute clear manipulations which are unacceptable on ethical grounds
Fluid, electrolyte disturbances; osteoporosis; spontaneous fractures; tendon rupture; endocrine changes; impaired wound healing; thin fragile skin; peptic ulcer with possible perforation; others, consult literature	Oral corticosteroids are banned

ANY RELATED COMPOUND TO THE EXAMPLES LISTED ABOVE ARE ALSO BANNED.

Brand (Generic) Manufacturer	IOC Category	Indications	Contraindications
Lem Plus Capsules (Paracetamol, *caffeine*, **phenyl-ephrine**) *Wallis*	1A	Colds and flu	
Lemsip Cold Relief (Paracetamol, **phenylephrine,** sodium citrate) *Reckitt & Colman*	1A	Colds, headache, body aches and pains	
Levobunolol	1D		Refer to Brand(s): Betagan
Levophed (Noradrenaline) *Sterling Winthrop*	1A	Restoration of blood pressure (emergency use) in cases of acute hypotension	Hypovolaemia (except as emergency measure); mesenteric or peripheral vascular thrombosis; cyclopropane and halothane anaesthesia; profound hypoxia or hypercarbia
LH	1F		Refer to Brand(s): Gonadotraphon L.H., Profasi
Local anaesthetics	3C		
Lopresor, Lopresor SR (Metoprolol) *Geigy*	1D	Cardioselective β_1-blocker. Hypertension; angina pectoris; suspected or definite myocardial infarction; migraine prophylaxis; thyrotoxicosis (adjunct)	2nd or 3rd degree heart block; cardiogenic shock; uncontrolled heart failure; sinus bradycardia; sick-sinus syndrome; severe peripheral arterial disease
Lopresoretic (Metoprolol, chlorthalidone) *Geigy*	1D, 1E	Mild and moderate hypertension	2nd or 3rd degree heart block; uncontrolled heart failure; severe bradycardia; cardiogenic shock; marked renal insufficiency; lithium therapy
Marcain with Adrenaline (Bupivacaine, adrenaline) *Astra*	3C	Local anaesthesia	Intravenous regional anaesthesia; thyrotoxicosis; severe heart disease

THE DOPING DEFINITION OF THE IOC MEDICAL COMMISSION IS BASED ON THE BANNING OF PHARMACEUTICAL CLASSES OF AGENTS.

Adverse Reactions	Comments
Hypertension; bradycardia; headache; peripheral ischaemia; cardiac arrhythmias	
	Subject to certain restrictions, refer to Explanations of Doping Classes and Methods Plain local anaesthetics are acceptable (when medically justified); those with adrenaline are not Written notification must be submitted immediately to the IOC Medical Commission
Gastrointestinal upset; hypotension; bradycardia; cold extremities; headache; sleep disturbances	Misuse in some sports where physical activity is of little or no importance; the IOC Medical Commission reserves the right to test those sports which it deems are appropriate
Gastrointestinal upset; sleep disturbances; exertional tiredness; cold extremities; bradycardia; bronchospasm; heart failure; manifest latent gout or diabetes; skin rash; dry eyes	Deliberate attempts to reduce weight artificially in order to compete in lower weight classes or to dilute urine constitute clear manipulations which are unacceptable on ethical grounds Misuse in some sports where physical activity is of little or no importance; the IOC Medical Commission reserves the right to test those sports which it deems are appropriate
CNS disturbances incl. tongue numbness; lightheadedness; dizziness; blurred vision; muscle twitch; drowsiness; convulsions; unconsciousness; respiratory arrest; depression of cardiac conduction	

· **ANY RELATED COMPOUND TO THE EXAMPLES LISTED ABOVE ARE ALSO BANNED.**

Brand (Generic) Manufacturer	IOC Category	Indications	Contraindications
Mackenzies Decongestant (Methylephedrine, menthol, paracetamol, guaiphenesin, chlorpheniramine) *Cox*	1A	Catarrh, sinus congestion; hayfever	
Marijuana	3B		
Mazindol	1A		Refer to Brand(s): Teronac
Medihaler Epi (Adrenaline) *3M Health Care*	1A	Relief of bronchospasm due to asthma, emphysema, drug sensitivity, injected allergens, urticaria and other allergic manifestations	Cardiac disease; hypertension; hyperthyroidism
Medihaler Iso (Isoprenaline) *3M Health Care*	1A	Acute relief of bronchospasm due to asthma, emphysema, etc.	Severe cardiac disease; pre-existing ventricular arrhythmia; severe hypertension; hyperthyroidism
Medocodene (Codeine, paracetamol) *Medo*	1B	Moderate pain and fever	
Medrone (Methyl-prednisolone) *Upjohn*	3D	Steroid responsive conditions	Systemic fungal infections; live virus immunisation
Mefruside	1E		Refer to Brand(s): Baycaron
Meltus Dry Cough Elixir (Pseudoephedrine, dextromethorphan) *Cupal*	1A	Dry cough	Asthmatics
Meptazinol	1B		Refer to Brand(s): Meptid
Meptid (Meptazinol) *Wyeth*	1B	Short-term treatment of moderate pain	

THE DOPING DEFINITION OF THE IOC MEDICAL COMMISSION IS BASED ON THE BANNING OF PHARMACEUTICAL CLASSES OF AGENTS.

Adverse Reactions	Comments
	Subject to certain restrictions, refer Doping Classes and Methods, Explanations
Gastric pain; dry mouth; palpitations; nervousness; tolerance	
Dry mouth; palpitations; nervousness	
Dependence, tolerance; nausea, vomiting, constipation; dizziness, drowsiness	
Sodium and fluid retention; osteoporosis; aseptic necrosis; peptic ulcer with possible perforation; impaired wound healing, thin fragile skin; psychic derangements; hypothalamic pituitary adrenal axis suppression; decreased carbohydrate tolerance; increased intraocular and intracranial pressure; cataracts; muscle weakness, myopathy; tendon rupture; growth suppression	Oral corticosteroids are banned
Drowsiness	
Nausea, vomiting, diarrhoea; dizziness; increased sweating; abdominal pain; rash; vertigo; headache; somnolence; dyspepsia	

ANY RELATED COMPOUND TO THE EXAMPLES LISTED ABOVE ARE ALSO BANNED.

Brand (Generic) Manufacturer	IOC Category	Indications	Contraindications
Mesterolone	1C		Refer to Brand(s): Pro-viron
Metaraminol	1A		Refer to Brand(s): Aramine
Metenix (Metolazone) *Hoechst*	1E	Mild to moderate hypertension; oedema	Electrolyte deficiency; anuria; hepatic precoma
Methadone	1B		Refer to Brand(s): Physeptone
Methoxamine	1A		Refer to Brand(s): Vasoxine
Methyclothiazide	1E		Refer to Brand(s): Enduron
Methylephedrine	1A		Refer to Brand(s): Mackenzies Decongestant
Methylphenidate	1A		Refer to Brand(s): Ritalin
Methyl-prednisolone	3D		Refer to Brand(s): Depo-Medrone Medrone, Min-I-Mix Methylprednisolone, Solu-Medrone
Metipranolol	1D		Refer to Brand(s): Minims Metipranolol
Metolazone	1E		Refer to Brand(s): Metenix
Metoprolol	1D		Refer to Brand(s): Betaloc, Betaloc SA, Co-Betaloc, Lopresor, Lopresor SR, Lopresoretic, Metoprolol
Metoprolol (Metoprolol) *APS* *Cox* *Kerfoot*	1D	Hypertension	2nd or 3rd degree heart block; uncontrolled heart failure; sinus bradycardia; sick sinus syndrome; severe peripheral arterial disease; cardiogenic shock
Midamor (Amiloride) *Morson*	1E	Potassium sparing diuretic. Hypertension; congestive heart failure; hepatic cirrhosis with ascites	Hyperkalaemia; concomitant potassium supplements or potassium sparing drugs/ diuretics; anuria; acute renal failure; severe progressive renal disease; diabetic nephropathy; children

THE DOPING DEFINITION OF THE IOC MEDICAL COMMISSION IS BASED ON THE BANNING OF PHARMACEUTICAL CLASSES OF AGENTS.

Adverse Reactions	Comments
Headache; anorexia, vomiting, abdominal discomfort; muscle cramps; dizziness; fluid, electrolyte disturbance	Deliberate attempts to reduce weight artificially in order to compete in lower weight classes or to dilute urine constitute clear manipulations which are unacceptable on ethical grounds
Headache; dizziness; vertigo; fatigue; nausea; diarrhoea; gastralgia; sleep disturbances; bradycardia; skin rash; consult literature	Misuse in some sports where physical activity is of little or no importance; the IOC Medical Commission reserves the right to test those sports which it deems are appropriate
Hyperkalaemia; nausea; anorexia; abdominal pain; flatulence; mild skin rash; headache; weakness; fatigability; back pain; chest pain; neck/shoulder ache; pain in extremities; angina pectoris; orthostatic hypotension; arrhythmia; palpitation; vomiting, diarrhoea, constipation; gastrointestinal bleeding; jaundice; thirst; dyspepsia, heartburn, flatulence; dry mouth; alopecia; muscle cramps; joint pain; dizziness, vertigo; paraesthesia; tremors; encephalopathy; nervousness, mental confusion, insomnia; decreased libido; depression; somnolence; cough, dyspnoea; nasal congestion; visual disturbances, increased intraocular pressure; tinnitus; impotence; polyuria, dysuria, bladder spasms, frequency of micturition	Deliberate attempts to reduce weight artificially in order to compete in lower weight classes or to dilute urine constitute clear manipulations which are unacceptable on ethical grounds

ANY RELATED COMPOUND TO THE EXAMPLES LISTED ABOVE ARE ALSO BANNED.

Brand (Generic) Manufacturer	IOC Category	Indications	Contraindications
Midrid (Isometheptene, paracetamol) *Shire*	1A	Migraine treatment	Severe renal, hepatic, cardiac disease; severe hypertension; glaucoma; concomitant MAOI therapy
Migraleve (Pink) (Codeine, buclizine, paracetamol) *Charwell*	1B	Migraine	
Migraleve (Yellow) (Codeine, paracetamol) *Charwell*	1B	Migraine	
Migralift (Pink) (Codeine, paracetamol) *International*	1B	Migraine attack treatment	
Migralift (Yellow) (Codeine, paracetamol) *International*	1A	Migraine attack treatment	
Min-I-Jet Adrenaline (Adrenaline) *IMS*	1A	Acute anaphylaxis (emergency treatment)	
Min-I-Jet Isoprenaline (Isoprenaline) *IMS*	1A	Heart block, severe bradycardia	
Min-I-Jet Lignocaine HCl with Adrenaline (Lignocaine, **adrenaline)** *IMS*	1A	Local or regional anaesthesia	Anaesthesia of fingers, toes, tip of nose, ears, penis; IV admin
Min-I-Mix Methyl- prednisolone (Methylpred- nisolone) *IMS*	3D	Corticosteroid responsive conditions	Systemic fungal infections; cerebral oedema in malaria; live virus immunisation

THE DOPING DEFINITION OF THE IOC MEDICAL COMMISSION IS BASED ON THE BANNING OF PHARMACEUTICAL CLASSES OF AGENTS.

Adverse Reactions	Comments
Dizziness	
Drowsiness	
Drowsiness	
Anxiety; tremor; tachycardia, arrhythmia; dry mouth; cold extremities	
Tachycardia; arrhythmias; hypotension; sweating; tremor; headache	
Inadvertent subarachnoid injection may lead to cardiovascular collapse, CNS depression, respiratory arrest More common reactions incl. nervousness, dizziness, blurred vision, tremor, drowsiness, tinnitus, numbness, disorientation, nausea, vomiting; see product literature	
Sodium, fluid retention; muscle weakness, myopathy; osteoporosis; tendon rupture; aseptic necrosis; peptic ulcer with possible perforation; impaired wound healing, thin fragile skin; growth suppression; decreased carbohydrate tolerance; cataracts; increased intraocular, intracranial pressure; psychic derangements; hypothalamic pituitary adrenal axis suppression	Parenteral corticosteroids are banned

ANY RELATED COMPOUND TO THE EXAMPLES LISTED ABOVE ARE ALSO BANNED.

Brand (Generic) Manufacturer	IOC Category	Indications	Contraindications
Minims Metipranolol (Metipranolol) *Smith & Nephew*	1D	Raised intra-ocular pressure	Obstructive airways disease; cardiac failure
Minims Phenylephrine (Phenylephrine) *Smith & Nephew*	1A	Mydriatic	Cardiac disease; hypertension; aneurysms; thyrotoxicosis; insulin dependent diabetes; tachycardia; concomitant MAOIs; glaucoma prone patients
Moducren (Hydrochloro-thiazide, amiloride, timolol) *Morson*	1D, 1E	Mild to moderate hypertension	Bronchial asthma; severe chronic obstructive pulmonary disease; sinus bradycardia; 2nd or 3rd degree heart block; overt cardiac failure; right ventricular failure secondary to pulmonary hypertension; significant cardiomegaly; cardiogenic shock; hyperkalaemia; anuria; acute or chronic renal insufficiency; severe progressive renal disease; diabetic nephropathy; hyperuraemia; diabetes mellitus; myocardial depressing anaesthetics; concomitant potassium supplements or potassium sparing drugs/diuretics
Moduret 25 (Amiloride, hydro-chlorothiazide) *Du Pont*	1E	Hypertension; congestive heart failure; hepatic cirrhosis with ascites	Hyperkalaemia; concomitant potassium or potassium sparing drugs/diuretics; anuria; acute renal failure; severe progressive renal disease; severe hepatic failure; hepatic precoma; Addison's disease; hypercalcaemia; concomitant lithium; diabetic nephropathy; hyperuraemia; children
Moduretic (Amiloride, hydro-chlorothiazide) *Du Pont*	1E	Potassium sparing diuretic. Hypertension; congestive heart failure; hepatic cirrhosis with ascites	Hyperkalaemia; concomitant potassium supplements or potassium sparing drugs/diuretics; anuria, acute renal failure, severe progressive renal disease; severe hepatic failure; hepatic precoma; Addison's disease; hypercalcaemia; concurrent lithium; diabetic nephropathy; hyperuricaemia; diabetes mellitus
Monocor (Bisoprolol) *Lederle*	1D	Hypertension; angina pectoris	Untreated cardiac failure; cardiogenic shock; sino-atrial block; 2nd or 3rd degree heart block; bradycardia; extreme hypotension
Monovent (Terbutaline) *Lagap*	1A	Relief of bronchospasm in bronchopulmonary conditions	Any condition of mother on fetus in which prolongation of pregnancy is hazardous

THE DOPING DEFINITION OF THE IOC MEDICAL COMMISSION IS BASED ON THE BANNING OF PHARMACEUTICAL CLASSES OF AGENTS.

Adverse Reactions	Comments
Systemic side effects possible	Misuse in some sports where physical activity is of little or no importance; the IOC Medical Commission reserves the right to test those sports which it deems are appropriate
Pain on instillation; possible palpitation, tachycardia, extrasystoles, cardiac arrhythmias, hypertension	
Complex: refer products with individual components for details or consult literature	Deliberate attempts to reduce weight artificially in order to compete in lower weight classes or to dilute urine constitute clear manipulations which are unacceptable on ethical grounds Misuse in some sports where physical activity is of little or no importance; the IOC Medical Commission reserves the right to test those sports which it deems are appropriate
Fluid, electrolyte disturbances; headache; fatigue, malaise; chest pain; back pain; syncope; cardiovascular disturbances; gastrointestinal upset; rash; CNS and psychiatric disturbances; impotence	Deliberate attempts to reduce weight artificially in order to compete in lower weight classes or to dilute urine constitute clear manipulations which are unacceptable on ethical grounds
Anorexia, nausea, vomiting, abdominal fullness, gastric irritation, cramping, pain, constipation, diarrhoea; dry mouth and thirst; paraesthesias; transient blurred vision; inflammation of a salivary gland; dizziness, vertigo, weakness, fatigability; muscle cramps; orthostatic hypotension; skin rash, pruritus; minor psychiatric disturbances; transient visual disturbances; haematological disturbances; purpura; rash; vasculitis; fever; respiratory distress; headache; restlessness; jaundice; pancreatitis; xanthopsia; hyperglycaemia; glycosuria; hyperuricaemia	Deliberate attempts to reduce weight artificially in order to compete in lower weight classes or to dilute urine constitute clear manipulations which are unacceptable on ethical grounds
Lassitude; dizziness; mild headache; perspiration; aggravation of intermittent claudication; skin rash; dry eyes; sleep disturbances	Misuse in some sports where physical activity is of little or no importance; the IOC Medical Commission reserves the right to test those sports which it deems are appropriate
Tremor; tonic cramp; palpitations; other less common reactions	Terbutaline via inhalation only is permitted; oral and injectable forms are banned

ANY RELATED COMPOUND TO THE EXAMPLES LISTED ABOVE ARE ALSO BANNED.

Brand (Generic) Manufacturer	IOC Category	Indications	Contraindications
Morphine	1B		Refer to Brand(s): Collis Browne's Mixture, Collis Browne's Tablets, Cyclimorph, Diocalm, Enterosan, IMS Morphine, Jacksons Pastilles, MST Continus, Nepenthe, Opazimes, Oramorp, T&R Gee's Linctus, Wig Gee's
MST Continus (Morphine) *Napp*	1B	Severe pain, prolonged relief	Respiratory depression; obstructive airways disease; acute hepatic disease; pre-op admin; MAOIs (concomitant or within 14 days); pregnancy; children
Mucron Tablets (Paracetamol, **phenylpropanol-amine**) *Ciba*	1A	Sinus pain, congestion; nasal congestion; catarrh	
Nadolol	1D		Refer to Brand(s): Corgard, Corgaretic
Nalbuphine	1B		Refer to Brand(s): Nubain
Nandrolone	1C		Refer to Brand(s): Deca-Durabolin, Deca-Durabolin 100, Durabolin
Narphen (Phenazocine) *Smith & Nephew*	1B	Severe pain	Coma; convulsive disorders; delirium tremens; myxoedema; alcoholism; respiratory depression; obstructive airways disease; MAOIs (concomitant or within 14 days)
Natrilix (Indapamide) *Servier*	1E	Essential hypertension	Anuria; progressive and severe oliguria; severe hepatic impairment
Navidrex (Cyclopenthiazide) *Ciba*	1E	Thiazide diuretic. Mild to moderate hypertension; acute and chronic heart failure; oedema	Anuria, severe renal and hepatic failure; refractory hypokalaemia, hyponatraemia, hypercalcaemia, hyperuricaemia; Addison's disease; lithium therapy
Navidrex-K (Cyclopenthiazide, potassium) *Ciba*	1E	As for Navidrex, plus potassium conservation	As for Navidrex, plus concomitant potassium supplements or potassium sparing drugs/diuretics
Navispare (Cyclopenthiazide, **amiloride**) *Ciba*	1E	Hypertension (mild to moderate)	Anuria; severe hepatic, renal disease; electrolyte imbalance incl. hyperkalaemia; Addison's disease; diabetic nephropathy; concomitant potassium supplements or potassium sparing drugs/diuretics; concomitant lithium

THE DOPING DEFINITION OF THE IOC MEDICAL COMMISSION IS BASED ON THE BANNING OF PHARMACEUTICAL CLASSES OF AGENTS.

Adverse Reactions	Comments
Tolerance, dependence; gastrointestinal upset	Pain of the severity to necessitate narcotic analgesia (with the risk of drug dependence), should prevent sports participation
Lightheadedness, dizziness; nausea, vomiting, constipation; pruritus; mouth dryness; sweating; hypotension; respiratory depression; tolerance, dependence	Pain of the severity to necessitate narcotic analgesia (with the risk of drug dependence), should prevent sports participation
Headache; muscle cramps; gastrointestinal disturbances; electrolyte imbalance (hypokalaemia, hypochloraemia, hyponatraemia)	Deliberate attempts to reduce weight artificially in order to compete in lower weight classes or to dilute urine constitute clear manipulations which are unacceptable on ethical grounds
Fluid and electrolyte disturbances; postural hypotension; cardiac arrhythmias; nausea, vomiting, bowel irregularity; dizziness; sleep disturbances; hypersensitivity reactions	Deliberate attempts to reduce weight artificially in order to compete in lower weight classes or to dilute urine constitute clear manipulations which are unacceptable on ethical grounds
As for Navidrex	Deliberate attempts to reduce weight artificially in order to compete in lower weight classes or to dilute urine constitute clear manipulations which are unacceptable on ethical grounds
GI upset; skin reactions; blood dyscrasias; gout; fatigue; consult literature	Deliberate attempts to reduce weight artificially in order to compete in lower weight classes or to dilute urine constitute clear manipulations which are unacceptable on ethical grounds

ANY RELATED COMPOUND TO THE EXAMPLES LISTED ABOVE ARE ALSO BANNED.

Brand (Generic) Manufacturer	IOC Category	Indications	Contraindications
Neo-Naclex **(Bendrofluazide)** *Duncan Flockhart*	1E	Essential hypertension; oedema	Severe renal or hepatic failure; Addison's disease; diabetic ketoacidosis; hypercalcaemia; concomitant lithium
Neo-Naclex-K **(Bendrofluazide,** potassium) *Duncan Flockhart*	1E	As for Neo-Naclex, plus potassium conservation	As for Neo-Naclex, plus concomitant potassium or potassium sparing drugs/ diuretics
Nepenthe **(Morphine)** *Evans*	1B	Severe pain	Respiratory depression; obstructive airways disease; MAOIs (concomitant or within 14 days)
Nephril **(Polythiazide)** *Pfizer*	1E	Hypertension; oedema	Anuria
Nirolex Expectorant **(Ephedrine** , guaiphenesin) *Boots*	1A	Cough	
Noradran (Diphenhydramine, diprophylline, **ephedrine,** guaiphenesin) *Norma*	1A	Decongestant	
Norditropin **(Somatropin** = **growth hormone)** *Novo Nordisk*	1F	Treatment of short stature prior to epiphyseal fusion due to an inadequate secretion of growth hormone	Active tumour
Normetic **(Amiloride,** **hydrochloro-** **thiazide)** *Abbott*	1E	Hypertension; oedema; congestive heart failure; hepatic cirrhosis with ascites; with potassium conservation	Hyperkalaemia; hypercalcaemia; concomitant potassium supplements or potassium conserving drugs/diuretics; acute renal failure, severe progressive renal disease; diabetic nephropathy; hepatic failure; Addison's disease; anuria; hyperuraemia; lithium
Nubain **(Nalbuphine)** *Du Pont*	1B	Moderate to severe pain	
Numotac **(Isoetharine)** *3M Health Care*	1A	Bronchospasm relief	Thyrotoxicosis

THE DOPING DEFINITION OF THE IOC MEDICAL COMMISSION IS BASED ON THE BANNING OF PHARMACEUTICAL CLASSES OF AGENTS.

Adverse Reactions	Comments
Electrolyte, fluid disturbances; disturbances of acid-base balance, lipids, glucose and uric acid levels; thirst, polyuria; weakness, dizziness; muscle cramps; reversible impotence; gastrointestinal upset; skin rash; blood dyscrasias	Deliberate attempts to reduce weight artificially in order to compete in lower weight classes or to dilute urine constitute clear manipulations which are unacceptable on ethical grounds
As for Neo-Naclex	Deliberate attempts to reduce weight artificially in order to compete in lower weight classes or to dilute urine constitute clear manipulations which are unacceptable on ethical grounds
Tolerance, dependence; nausea, vomiting	Pain of the severity to necessitate narcotic analgesia (with the risk of drug dependence), should prevent sports participation
Fluid, electrolyte disturbances; gastrointestinal upset; CNS disturbances; blood dyscrasias; hypotension; muscle spasm, weakness; restlessness	Deliberate attempts to reduce weight artificially in order to compete in lower weight classes or to dilute urine constitute clear manipulations which are unacceptable on ethical grounds
Drowsiness	
Antibody formation	Misuse of growth hormone in sport is deemed to be unethical and dangerous
Fluid, electrolyte disturbances; orthostatic hypotension; muscle cramps; fatigue, weakness; dizziness, vertigo; salivary gland inflammation; transient blurred vision; paraesthesia; thirst, dry mouth; gastrointestinal upset; others, consult literature	Deliberate attempts to reduce weight artificially in order to compete in lower weight classes or to dilute urine constitute clear manipulations which are unacceptable on ethical grounds
Dependence; sedation; sweating; nausea, vomiting; dizziness; dry mouth; vertigo; headache	Pain of the severity to necessitate narcotic analgesia (with the risk of dependence), should prevent sports participation
Cardiovascular effects incl. vasodilation, tachycardia, palpitation, lightheadedness; fine tremor; nervousness; headache; insomnia; rebound bronchoconstriction	

ANY RELATED COMPOUND TO THE EXAMPLES LISTED ABOVE ARE ALSO BANNED.

Brand (Generic) Manufacturer	IOC Category	Indications	Contraindications
Omnopon (**Papaveretum**) Roche	1B	Relief of post-op and severe chronic pain; pre-op medication; severe chronic pain	Respiratory depression; obstructive airways disease; comatose patients; MAOIs (concomitant or within 14 days)
Omnopon-Scopolamine (Hyoscine, **papaveretum**) Roche	1B	Pre-anaesthetic medication	
Opazimes (**Morphine,** aluminium hydroxide, kaolin, belladonna) Rybar	1B	Diarrhoea; mild gastroenteritis; stomach upset	
Operidine (**Phenoperidine**) Janssen	1B	Narcotic analgesia; supplement in anaesthesia; neuroleptanalgesia (with a neuroleptic); respiratory depression/analgesia where prolonged assisted ventilation required	Obstructive airways disease; respiratory depression; MAOIs (concomitant or within 14 days); myasthenia gravis
Opium	1B		Refer Brand(s): Gee's Linctus Pastilles, T&R Gee's Linctus, Wig Gee's
Opium	1B	*Analgesic and narcotic action; may be given as Aromatic Chalk with Opium Mixture for diarrhoea*	
Oradexon (**Dexamethasone**) Organon	3D	Corticosteroid responsive conditions incl. cerebral oedema; diagnostic testing of adrenocortical hyperfunction	Systemic fungal infection
Oramorph (**Morphine**) Boehringer Ingelheim	1B	Relief of severe pain	Respiratory depression; obstructive airways disease; acute hepatic disease; acute alcoholism; head injuries; coma; convulsive disorders; raised intracranial pressure; MAOIs (concomitant or within 14 days)
Orciprenaline	1A		Refer to Brand(s): Alupent
Oxprenolol	1D		Refer to Brand(s): Apsolox, (Oxprenolol), Oxyprenix 160-SR, Slow-Pren, Slow-Trasicor, Trasicor, Trasidrex

THE DOPING DEFINITION OF THE IOC MEDICAL COMMISSION IS BASED ON THE BANNING OF PHARMACEUTICAL CLASSES OF AGENTS.

Adverse Reactions	Comments
Impaired alertness; tolerance, dependence; nausea, vomiting; confusion; constipation	Pain of the severity to necessitate narcotic analgesia (with the risk of drug dependence), should prevent sports participation
Impaired alertness; tolerance, dependence; nausea, vomiting; confusion; constipation; mouth dryness, thirst; ocular changes (incl. photophobia); flushing; skin dryness; tachycardia; inability to urinate	Pain of the severity to necessitate narcotic analgesia (with the risk of drug dependence), should prevent sports participation
Respiratory depression; muscle rigidity; dependence; bradycardia; see product literature	Pain of the severity to necessitate narcotic analgesia (with the risk of drug dependence), should prevent sports participation
Dependence, abuse	*Pain of the severity to necessitate narcotic analgesia (with the risk of drug dependence), should prevent sports participation*
Sodium and fluid retention; peptic ulcer with possible perforation; muscle weakness and myopathy; osteoporosis; tendon rupture; aseptic necrosis; impaired wound healing, thin fragile skin; growth suppression; decreased carbohydrate tolerance; psychic derangements; increased intraocular and intracranial pressure; cataracts; hypothalamic pituitary adrenal axis suppression	Oral corticosteroids are banned
Dependence, tolerance; nausea, vomiting; impaired alertness	Pain of the severity to necessitate narcotic analgesia (with the risk of drug dependence), should prevent sports participation

ANY RELATED COMPOUND TO THE EXAMPLES LISTED ABOVE ARE ALSO BANNED.

Brand (Generic) Manufacturer	IOC Category	Indications	Contraindications
Oxprenolol (Oxprenolol) *Cox Evans Kerfoot*	1D	Angina pectoris; hypertension; cardiac arrhythmias; short-term relief of somatic symptoms of anxiety; other cardiovascular indications, consult literature	2nd or 3rd degree heart block; marked bradycardia; uncontrolled heart failure; cardiogenic shock; sick-sinus syndrome; bronchial asthma; anaesthesia with ether, chloroform
Oxymetholone	1C		Refer to Brand(s): Anapolon 50
Oxyprenix 160-SR (Oxprenolol) *Ashbourne*	1B	Angina pectoris; hypertension; cardiac arrhythmias; short-term relief of somatic symptoms of anxiety; other cardiovascular indications, consult literature	2nd or 3rd degree heart block; marked bradycardia; uncontrolled heart failure; cardiogenic shock; sick-sinus syndrome; bronchial asthma; anaesthesia with ether, chloroform
Palfium (Dextromoramide) *Boehringer Mannheim*	1B	Relief of severe pain	Respiratory depression; chronic obstructive airways disease; childbirth; MAOIs (concomitant or within 14 days)
Pamergan P100 (Pethidine, promethazine) *Martindale*	1B	Pre-anaesthetic medication; obstetrical analgesia and amnesia; management of severe pain	Severe hepatic disease; post cholecystectomy; biliary colic; increased intracranial pressure; respiratory depression; chronic obstructive airways disease; MAOIs (concomitant or within 14 days)
Panadeine Co (Codeine, paracetamol) *Sterling Health*	1B	Moderate pain and fever	
Panerel (Paracetamol, *caffeine*, codeine) *Cox*	1B	Moderate pain and fever	
Papaveretum	1B		Refer to Brand(s): Aspav, Omnopon, Omnopon-Scopolamine
Paracodol (Codeine, paracetamol) *Fisons*	1B	Moderate pain and fever	
Parahypon (Codeine, *caffeine*, paracetamol) *Wellcome*	1B	Moderate pain and fever	

THE DOPING DEFINITION OF THE IOC MEDICAL COMMISSION IS BASED ON THE BANNING OF PHARMACEUTICAL CLASSES OF AGENTS.

Adverse Reactions	Comments
Hypotension; bradycardia; cold extremities; headache; sleep disturbances; dizziness, drowsiness; insomnia; excitement; dry mouth; vision disturbances; keratoconjunctivitis; loss of libido; gastrointestinal disturbances; bronchospasm; dyspnoea; heart failure	Misuse in some sports where physical activity is of little or no importance; the IOC Medical Commission reserves the right to test those sports which it deems are appropriate
Hypotension; bradycardia; cold extremities; headache; sleep disturbances; dizziness, drowsiness; insomnia; excitement; dry mouth; vision disturbances; keratoconjunctivitis; loss of libido; gastrointestinal disturbances; bronchospasm; dyspnoea; heart failure	Misuse in some sports where physical activity is of little or no importance; the IOC Medical Commission reserves the right to test those sports which it deems are appropriate
Dependence, tolerance; dizziness; nausea, vomiting; perspiration; respiratory depression	Pain of the severity to necessitate narcotic analgesia (with the risk of drug dependence), should prevent sports participation
Mouth dryness; blurred vision; disorientation, dizziness; tolerance, dependence	Pain of the severity to necessitate narcotic analgesia (with the risk of drug dependence), should prevent sports participation
Dependence, tolerance; nausea, vomiting, constipation; dizziness, drowsiness	
Dependence, tolerance; nausea, vomiting, constipation; dizziness, drowsiness	
Dependence, tolerance; nausea, vomiting, constipation; dizziness, drowsiness	
Dependence, tolerance; nausea, vomiting, constipation; dizziness, drowsiness	

ANY RELATED COMPOUND TO THE EXAMPLES LISTED ABOVE ARE ALSO BANNED.

Brand (Generic) Manufacturer	IOC Category	Indications	Contraindications
Parake (Paracetamol, **codeine)** *Galen*	1B	Moderate pain and fever	
Paramol (**Dihydrocodeine,** paracetamol) *Duncan Flockart*	1B	Mild to moderate pain	Respiratory depression; chronic obstructive airways disease
Pardale (**Codeine, *caffeine*,** paracetamol) *Martindale*	1B	Moderate pain and fever	
Paxalgesic (**Dextropropoxyphene,** paracetamol) *Steinhard*	1B	Management of mild to moderate pain	Alcohol; suicidal or emotionally unstable individuals
Pemoline	1A		Refer to Brand(s): Prowess, Volital
Penbutolol	1D		Refer to Brand(s): Lasipressin
Pentazocine	1B		Refer to Brand(s): Fortagesic, Fortral, Pentazocine
Pethidine	1B		Refer to Brand(s): Pamergan P100
Phenazocine	1B		Refer to Brand(s): Narphen
Phenoperidine	1B		Refer to Brand(s): Operidine
Phensedyl (**Codeine,** promethazine) *May & Baker*	1A	Unproductive cough	MAOI treatment
Phentermine	1A		Refer to Brand(s): Duromine, Ionamine
Phenylephrine	1A		Refer to Brand(s): Beecham's Catarrh, Beecham's Powders Caps, Betnovate Rectal, Bronchilator, Cabdrivers, Coldrex Powd, Dimotapp, Dristan Tabs, Fenox, Flurex Caps, Flurex Tabs, Isopto Frin, Lem Plus Caps, LemSip, Minims Phenylephrine, Phenylephrine Inj 1%, Uniflu, Vibrocil, Vicks

THE DOPING DEFINITION OF THE IOC MEDICAL COMMISSION IS BASED ON THE BANNING OF PHARMACEUTICAL CLASSES OF AGENTS.

Adverse Reactions	Comments
Dependence, tolerance; nausea, vomiting, constipation; dizziness, drowsiness	
Constipation, nausea; headache, dizziness	
Dependence, tolerance; nausea, vomiting, constipation; dizziness, drowsiness	
Dependence; dizziness; sedation; nausea, vomiting, constipation, abdominal pain; skin rash; lightheadedness; headache; weakness; euphoria, dysphonia, visual disturbances	Pain of the severity to necessitate narcotic analgesia (with the risk of drug dependence), should prevent sports participation
Drowsiness	

ANY RELATED COMPOUND TO THE EXAMPLES LISTED ABOVE ARE ALSO BANNED.

Brand (Generic) Manufacturer	IOC Category	Indications	Contraindications
Phenylephrine Injection 1% (Phenylephrine) *Boots*	1A	Acute hypotension	Severe hypertension, hyperthyroidism; myocardial infarction; pregnancy
Phenylpropanol-amine	1A		Refer to Brand(s): Aller-eze Plus, Benylin Day & Night (Daytime tablets), Contac 400, Day Nurse Capsules, Dimetapp, Eskornade, Junior Mucron, Moorefields Phenylephrine, Mucron Tablets, Procol, Sine-off, Sinutab, Triogesic, Triominic, Vicks Cold Care
Physeptone (Methadone) *Wellcome*	1B	Severe pain	Respiratory depression; chronic obstructive airways disease; MAOIs (concomitant or within 14 days); obstetric use
Pindolol	1D		Refer to Brand(s): Betadren, Viskaldix, Visken
Pirbuterol	1A		Refer to Brand(s): Exirel
Pirertanide	1E		Refer to Brand(s): Arelix
Polythiazide	1E		Refer to Brand(s): Nephril
Precortisyl, Precortisyl Forte (Prednisolone) *Roussel*	3D	Corticosteroid responsive states	Systemic fungal infections; peptic ulcer; osteoporosis
Predenema (Prednisolone) *Pharmax*	3D	Local treatment of ulcerative colitis	Peritonitis; fistulae; intestinal obstruction; bowel perforation
Predfoam (Prednisolone) *Pharmax*	3D	Treatment of proctitis, ulcerative colitis	Peritonitis; fistulae; intestinal obstruction; bowel perforation
Prednesol (Prednisolone) *Glaxo*	3D	Corticosteroid responsive conditions	Systemic infections; live virus immunisation
Prednisolone	3D		Refer to Brand(s): Deltacortril, Deltastab, Precortisyl, Predenema, Predfoam, Prednesol, Predsol, Predsol N, Sintisone

THE DOPING DEFINITION OF THE IOC MEDICAL COMMISSION IS BASED ON THE BANNING OF PHARMACEUTICAL CLASSES OF AGENTS.

Adverse Reactions	Comments
Hypertension; headache; palpitations, tachycardia, reflex bradycardia; vomiting; tingling, cool skin	
Dependence; euphoria; dizziness; drowsiness; vomiting, nausea; respiratory depression	Pain of the severity to necessitate narcotic analgesia (with the risk of drug dependence), should prevent sports participation
Sodium, fluid retention; peptic ulcer with possible perforation; impaired wound healing, thin fragile skin; decreased carbohydrate tolerance; growth suppression; muscle weakness, myopathy, aseptic necrosis, tendon rupture, osteoporosis; cataract, increased intraocular and intracranial pressure; psychic derangements; hypothalamic pituitary adrenal axis suppression	Oral corticosteroids are banned
Mask infection; thin fragile skin; impaired wound healing; possible systemic side effects	Topical rectal administration of corticosteroids is banned because the systemic blood levels of corticosteroids achieved via rectal administration are comparable to levels after oral ingestion
Mask infection; thin fragile skin; impaired wound healing; possible systemic side effects	Topical rectal administration of corticosteroids is banned because the systemic blood levels of corticosteroids achieved via rectal administration are comparable to levels after oral ingestion
Sodium, fluid retention; muscle weakness, myopathy; osteoporosis; aseptic necrosis; tendon rupture; peptic ulcer with possible perforation; impaired wound healing, thin fragile skin; decreased carbohydrate tolerance; growth suppression; cataracts; increased intracranial, intraocular pressure; psychic derangements; hypothalamic pituitary adrenal axis suppression	Oral corticosteroids are banned

ANY RELATED COMPOUND TO THE EXAMPLES LISTED ABOVE ARE ALSO BANNED.

Brand (Generic) Manufacturer	IOC Category	Indications	Contraindications
Prednisone	3D		Refer to Brand(s): Decortisyl
Predsol Retention Enema, Suppositories (Prednisolone) *Glaxo*	3D	Ulcerative colitis, Crohn's disease, local treatment	Primary infection by viruses or other microorganisms
Pregnyl (Chorionic gonadotrophin) *Organon*	1F	Male: hypogonadotrophic hypogonadism or delayed puberty, cryptorchism, deficient spermatogenesis Female: anovulatory sterility	Androgen dependent tumour
Prestim (Timolol, bendrofluazide) *Leo*	1D, 1E	Mild to moderate hypertension	Anuria, renal failure; uncontrolled heart failure; bradycardia; cardiogenic shock; bronchial asthma; chronic obstructive pulmonary disease; MAOIs (concomitant or within 14 days); myocardial depressant anaesthetics; concomitant lithium
Primoteston Depot (Testosterone) *Schering Health Care*	1C	Male: androgen deficiency Female: carcinoma of the breast	Carcinoma of prostate; pregnancy
Probenecid	2B		Refer to Brand(s): Benemid
Procol (Phenylpropanol-amine) *Wellcome*	1A	Cold symptoms	
Profasi (Chorionic gonadotrophin) *Serono*	1F	Infertility	Ovarian dysgenesis; absent uterus; premature menopause; tubal occlusion (unless undergoing IVF)
Prolintane	1A		Refer to Brand(s): Villescon
Propain (Codeine, *caffeine*, paracetamol, diphenhydramine) *Panpharma*	1B	Moderate pain and fever	

THE DOPING DEFINITION OF THE IOC MEDICAL COMMISSION IS BASED ON THE BANNING OF PHARMACEUTICAL CLASSES OF AGENTS.

Adverse Reactions	Comments
Systemic side effects possible	Topical rectal administration of corticosteroids is banned because the systemic blood levels of corticosteroids achieved via rectal administration are comparable to levels after oral ingestion
Skin rash; water, salt retention	Considered equivalent to the exogenous administration of testosterone
Gastrointestinal upset; dizziness; insomnia; sedation; depression; weakness; dyspnoea; bradycardia; heart block; bronchospasm; heart failure; fluid, electrolyte disturbances; muscle pain, fatigue; thirst; oliguria; skin rash; dry eyes; blood dyscrasias	Misuse in some sports where physical activity is of little or no importance; the IOC Medical Commission reserves the right to test those sports which it deems are appropriate. Deliberate attempts to reduce weight artificially in order to compete in lower weight classes or to dilute urine constitute clear manipulations which are unacceptable on ethical grounds
Salt, water retention; virilising effects in women; others, consult literature	Misused in sport, not only to attempt to increase muscle bulk, strength and power when used with increased food intake but also in lower doses and normal food intake to attempt to improve competitiveness. The definition of a positive result is: a ratio in urine of testosterone/epitestosterone >6
Hyperstimulation; multiple pregnancy; oedema; sexual precocity; local reaction at injection site	Considered equivalent to the exogenous administration of testosterone
Dependence, tolerance; nausea, vomiting, constipation; dizziness, drowsiness	

ANY RELATED COMPOUND TO THE EXAMPLES LISTED ABOVE ARE ALSO BANNED.

Brand (Generic) Manufacturer	IOC Category	Indications	Contraindications
Propine (Dipivefrin) *Allergan*	1A	Chronic open angle glaucoma	Narrow angle glaucoma
Propranolol	1D		Refer to Brand(s): Angilol, Apsolol, Bedranol, Berkolol, Cardinol, Half-Inderal LA, Inderal, Inderal LA, Inderetic, Inderex, (Propranolol)
Propranolol (Propranolol) *Cox Evans Kerfoot*	1D	Nonselective β-blocker. Hypertension, angina pectoris, cardiac arrhythmias (eg. anxiety tachycardia), essential tremor, phaeochromocytoma, hypertrophic subaortic stenosis; prophylaxis of migraine and recurrent vascular headaches; suspected or definite myocardial infarction	2nd or 3rd degree heart block; cardiogenic shock; bronchospasm; prolonged fasting; metabolic acidosis
Pro-viron Tablets (Mesterolone) *Schering*	1C	Androgen deficiency; male infertility, hypogonadism, disturbances of potency	Prostatic carcinoma
Prowess (Pemoline, testosterone, yohimbine) *Harley Street Supplies*	1A, 1C	Sexual impotence	
Pseudoephedrine	1A		Refer to Brand(s): Actifed, Benylin, Bonalin Dry Cough Elixir, Catarrh-Ex, Coldrex Tablets, Congesteze, Dimotane Co, Dimotane Co Paediatric, Dimotane Expectorant, Expulin, Flurex Bedtime Cold Remedy, Galpseud, Meltus Dry Cough Elixir, Robitussin Expectorant Plus, Sudafed, Sudafed Co, Sudafed Plus
Pulmo Baily (Codeine, guaiphenesin, phosphoric acid) *Chancellor*	1B	Symptomatic treatment of coughs, bronchial catarrh, colds, influenza, laryngitis, pharyngitis	
Rapifen (Alfentanil) *Janssen*	1B	Potent narcotic analgesic	Obstructive airways disease; respiratory depression; MAOIs (concurrent or within 14 days)
Recormon (Erythropoietin) *Boehringer Man*	1F, 2B	Correction of erythropoietin deficiency in dialysis patients with renal anaemia	

THE DOPING DEFINITION OF THE IOC MEDICAL COMMISSION IS BASED ON THE BANNING OF PHARMACEUTICAL CLASSES OF AGENTS.

Adverse Reactions	Comments
Tachycardia; arrhythmia; hypertension; burning; stinging	
Hypotension; bradycardia; cold extremities; headache; sleep disturbances; angina; dry eyes; skin rash	Misuse in some sports where physical activity is of little or no importance; the IOC Medical Commission reserves the right to test those sports which it deems are appropriate
	Misused in sport, not only to attempt to increase muscle bulk, strength and power when used with increased food intake but also in lower doses and normal food intake to attempt to improve competitiveness
	Misused in sport, not only to attempt to increase muscle bulk, strength and power when used with increased food intake but also in lower doses and normal food intake to attempt to improve competitiveness The definition of a positive result is: a ratio in urine of testosterone/epitestosterone > 6
	Cough and cold preparations which contain drugs of the narcotic analgesic class are banned
Respiratory depression; nausea, vomiting; dizziness; decreased blood pressure; bradycardia	Pain of the severity to necessitate narcotic analgesia (with the risk of drug dependence), should prevent sports participation
Flu-like symptoms incl. headache, weakness, aching joints, dizziness, lassitude; increased blood pressure; increased platelet count; increased blood viscosity; shunt thromboses; hyperkalaemia	.

ANY RELATED COMPOUND TO THE EXAMPLES LISTED ABOVE ARE ALSO BANNED.

Brand (Generic) Manufacturer	IOC Category	Indications	Contraindications
Reproterol	1A		Refer to Brand(s): Bronchodil
Restandol (Testosterone) *Organon*	1C	Testosterone replacement therapy in male hypogonadal disorders; osteoporosis due to androgenic deficiency	Prostatic, mammary carcinoma; hypercalciuria; hypercalcaemia; nephrotic syndrome; ischaemic heart disease; untreated congestive heart failure
Ritalin (Methylphenidate) *Ciba*	1A	Children >6 years with refractory hyperkinetic states	Marked anxiety, tension; severe angina pectoris; glaucoma; tachyarrhythmias; thyrotoxicosis; severe depression; epilepsy; concomitant pressor agents, MAOIs, tricyclic antidepressants
Ritrodrine	1A		Refer to Brand(s): Yutopar
Robitussin Expectorant Plus (Guaiphenesin, **pseudoephedrine**) *Whitehall*	1A	Nasal, chest congestion	
Rusyde (Frusemide) *CP Pharmaceuticals*	1E	Oedema	Hepatic precoma; electrolyte deficiency
Saizen (Somatropin = growth hormone) *Serono*	1F	Short stature resulting from growth failure caused by decreased or absent secretion of endogenous growth hormone	Closed epiphyses; recurrence or progression of an underlying cranial lesion; pregnancy, lactation
Salbulin Tablets (Salbutamol) *3M Health Care*	1A	Bronchospasm relief in chronic bronchitis in bronchial asthma, pulmonary emphysema	Concurrent β-blockers
Salbutamol	1A		Refer to Brand(s): Asmaven, Salbulin, Salbuvent (Tablets, Syrup, Injection, Infusion), Ventolin (Tablets, Syrup, Injection), Volmax
Salbuvent Tablets, Syrup, Injection, Infusion (Salbutamol) *Tillotts*	1A	Bronchospasm assoc. with asthma, bronchitis, emphysema	Premature labour assoc. with toxaemia or haemorrhage
Saluric (Chlorothiazide) *Merck*	1E	Oedema; hypertension	Anuria; severe renal, hepatic failure; Addison's disease; hypercalcaemia; concurrent lithium

THE DOPING DEFINITION OF THE IOC MEDICAL COMMISSION IS BASED ON THE BANNING OF PHARMACEUTICAL CLASSES OF AGENTS.

Adverse Reactions	Comments
Priapism; excessive sexual stimulation; precocious sexual development; increased frequency of erections; phallic enlargement, premature epiphyseal closure in pre-pubertal males; salt, water retention; oligospermia; decreased ejaculatory volume; voice change; virilisation	Misused in sport not only to attempt to increase muscle bulk, strength and power when used with increased food intake but also lower doses and normal food intake to attempt to improve competitiveness The definition of a positive result is: a ratio in urine of testosterone/epitestosterone >6
Dependence; nervousness; insomnia; anorexia; rare hypersensitivity reactions, nausea, dizziness, palpitations, headache, dyskinesia, drowsiness, skin rash; blood pressure, pulse rate changes	
Fluid, electrolyte disturbances; nausea; malaise; gastric upset; hyperuricaemia	Deliberate attempts to reduce weight artificially in order to compete in lower weight classes or to dilute urine constitute clear manipulations which are unacceptable on ethical grounds
Local reactions at inj. site; antibody formation	
Skeletal muscle tremor	Salbutamol via inhalation only is permitted; oral and injectable forms are banned
Skeletal tremor; increased heart rate	Salbutamol via inhalation only is permitted; oral and injectable forms are banned
Fluid, electrolyte disturbances; gastrointestinal, CNS, haematological, cardiovascular, metabolic and renal disturbances; complex, consult literature	Deliberate attempts to reduce weight artificially in order to compete in lower weight classes or to dilute urine constitute clear manipulations which are unacceptable on ethical grounds

ANY RELATED COMPOUND TO THE EXAMPLES LISTED ABOVE ARE ALSO BANNED.

Brand (Generic) Manufacturer	IOC Category	Indications	Contraindications
Saventrine **(Isoprenaline)** *Pharmax*	1A	Cardiogenic, endotoxic shock; acute Stokes-Adams attacks, cardiac emergencies; severe bradycardia; evaluation of congenital heart defects	Acute coronary disease
Secadrex **(Acebutolol, hydrochloro- thiazide)** *May & Baker*	1D, 1E	Mild and moderate hypertension	Cardiogenic shock; heart block; severe renal, hepatic failure; concomitant verapamil; insulin dependent diabetes; gout, hyperuricaemia; pregnancy
Sectral **(Acebutolol)** *May & Baker*	1D	Hypertension; angina pectoris; tachyarrhythmias	Cardiogenic shock; atrioventricular block; marked bradycardia; uncontrolled heart failure
Select-A-Jet **Dopamine** **(Dopamine)** *IMS*	1A	Cardiogenic shock	Tachyarrhythmia, phaeochromocytoma
Sepasil Esidrex **(Hydrochloro- thiazide,** reserpine) *Ciba*	1E	Hypertension	Depressive states; chronic nephritis
Sevredol **(Morphine)** *Napp*	1B	Narcotic analgesic. Severe pain	Respiratory depression; chronic obstructive airways disease; acute hepatic disease; acute alcoholism; raised intracranial pressure; head injuries; coma; convulsive disorders; MAOIs (concomitant or within 14 days)
Simplene **(Adrenaline)** *Smith & Nephew*	1A	Open angle glaucoma	Closed angle glaucoma; soft contact lenses
Sine-Off (Aspirin, chlorpheniramine, **phenylpropanol- amine)** *Wellcome*	1A	Sinus congestion and headache	
Sintisone **(Prednisolone)** *Farmitalia*	3D	Corticosteroid responsive disorders	Absolute: Herpes simplex; keratitis; acute psychoses Relative: active TB; peptic ulcer; Cushing's disease; renal insufficiency; severe diabetes; thromboembolic tendencies; osteoporosis; hypertension; uncontrolled systemic infections; viral or fungal infections; pregnancy

THE DOPING DEFINITION OF THE IOC MEDICAL COMMISSION IS BASED ON THE BANNING OF PHARMACEUTICAL CLASSES OF AGENTS.

Adverse Reactions	Comments
Palpitations; tremor; precordial pain; sweating; facial flushing; headache	
Hypotension; bradycardia; gastrointestinal upset; depression; skin rash; dry eyes; blood dyscrasias; consult literature	Misuse in some sports where physical activity is of little or no importance; the IOC Medical Commission reserves the right to test those sports which it deems are appropriate. Deliberate attempts to reduce weight artificially in order to compete in lower weight classes or to dilute urine constitute clear manipulations which are unacceptable on ethical grounds
Bradycardia; gastrointestinal upset; cold extremities; dizziness; headache; shortness of breath; nightmares; loss of libido; lethargy; skin rash; dry eyes	Misuse in some sports where physical activity is of little or no importance; the IOC Medical Commission reserves the right to test those sports which it deems are appropriate
Nausea, vomiting; peripheral vasoconstriction; hypotension, hypertension; tachycardia	
Anorexia, nausea; nasal congestion; lethargy, drowsiness; gastrointestinal upset; skin rash; photosensitivity; blood dyscrasias; orthostatic hypotension; weakness; fluid, electrolyte disturbances	Deliberate attempts to reduce weight artificially in order to compete in lower weight classes or to dilute urine constitute clear manipulations which are unacceptable on ethical grounds
Drowsiness; impaired alertness; respiratory depression; constipation, nausea, vomiting; dependence, tolerance	Pain of the severity to necessitate narcotic analgesia (with the risk of dependence), should prevent sports participation
Temporary blurred vision; smarting on instillation; eye pain, photophobia, redness; headache; browache; palpitations, tachycardia, increased blood pressure; extrasystoles, cardiac arrhythmias; faintness; sweating; pallor; trembling, perspiration	
Drowsiness	
Sodium, water retention; potassium excretion; aggravated endocrine diabetes mellitus; increased protein catabolism and uric acid secretion; redistribution of body fat; gastric disorders, possible exacerbation of gastroduodenal ulcers; CNS disturbances; increased susceptibility to infections; pituitary inhibition	Oral corticosteroids are banned

ANY RELATED COMPOUND TO THE EXAMPLES LISTED ABOVE ARE ALSO BANNED.

Brand (Generic) Manufacturer	IOC Category	Indications	Contraindications
Sinutab (Paracetamol, phenylpropanolamine) *Warner-Lambert*	1A	Nasal, sinus congestion; headache; pain	
Sloprolol (Propranolol) *CP Pharmaceuticals*	1D	Nonselective β-blocker. Hypertension, angina pectoris, cardiac arrhythmias (eg. anxiety tachycardia), essential tremor, phaeochromocytoma, hypertrophic subaortic stenosis; prophylaxis of migraine and recurrent vascular headaches; suspected or definite myocardial infarction	2nd or 3rd degree heart block; cardiogenic shock; bronchospasm; prolonged fasting; metabolic acidosis
Slow-Pren (Oxprenolol) *Norton*	1D	Angina pectoris; hypertension; cardiac arrhythmias; short-term relief of somatic symptoms of anxiety; other cardiovascular indications, consult literature	2nd or 3rd degree heart block; marked bradycardia; uncontrolled heart failure; cardiogenic shock; sick-sinus syndrome; bronchial asthma; anaesthesia with ether, chloroform
Slow-Trasicor (Oxprenolol) *Ciba*	1D		Refer: Trasicor
Solpadeine (Codeine, *caffeine*, paracetamol) *Sterling Winthrop*	1B	Analgesic. Moderate pain and fever	
Solpadol (Codeine, paracetamol) *Sterling Winthrop*	1B	Moderate pain and fever	
Solu-Cortef (Hydrocortisone) *Upjohn*	3D	Corticosteroid responsive conditions	Systemic fungal infections; live virus immunisation
Solu-Medrone (Methylprednisolone) *Upjohn*	3D	Corticosteroid responsive conditions	Systemic fungal infections; cerebral oedema in malaria; live virus immunisation
Somatropin	1F		Refer to Brand(s): Genotropin, Humatrope, Norditropin, Saizen

THE DOPING DEFINITION OF THE IOC MEDICAL COMMISSION IS BASED ON THE BANNING OF PHARMACEUTICAL CLASSES OF AGENTS.

Adverse Reactions	Comments
Hypotension; bradycardia; cold extremities; headache; sleep disturbances; angina; dry eyes; skin rash	Misuse in some sports where physical activity is of little or no importance; the IOC Medical Commission reserves the right to test those sports which it deems are appropriate
Hypotension; bradycardia; cold extremities; headache; sleep disturbances; dizziness, drowsiness; insomnia; excitement; dry mouth; vision disturbances; keratoconjunctivitis; loss of libido; gastrointestinal disturbances; bronchospasm; dyspnoea; heart failure	Misuse in some sports where physical activity is of little or no importance; the IOC Medical Commission reserves the right to test those sports which it deems are appropriate
Tolerance, dependence; nausea, vomiting, constipation; dizziness, drowsiness	
Tolerance, dependence; nausea, vomiting, constipation; dizziness, drowsiness	
Sodium, fluid retention; muscle weakness, myopathy; osteoporosis; tendon rupture; aseptic necrosis; peptic ulcer with possible perforation; impaired wound healing, thin fragile skin; growth suppression; decreased carbohydrate tolerance; cataracts; increased intraocular, intracranial pressure; psychic derangements; hypothalamic pituitary adrenal axis suppression	Parenteral corticosteroids are banned
Sodium, fluid retention; muscle weakness, myopathy; osteoporosis; tendon rupture; aseptic necrosis; peptic ulcer with possible perforation; impaired wound healing, thin fragile skin; growth suppression; decreased carbohydrate tolerance; cataracts; increased intraocular, intracranial pressure; psychic derangements; hypothalamic pituitary adrenal axis suppression	Parenteral corticosteroids are banned

ANY RELATED COMPOUND TO THE EXAMPLES LISTED ABOVE ARE ALSO BANNED.

Brand (Generic) Manufacturer	IOC Category	Indications	Contraindications
Sotacor (Sotalol) Bristol-Myers	1D	Hypertension; angina pectoris; thyrotoxicosis; cardiac arrhythmias; myocardial infarction	Bronchospasm; heart block; metabolic acidosis; diabetic ketoacidosis; cardiogenic shock
Sotalol	1D		Refer to Brand(s): Beta-Cardone, Sotacor, Sotazide, Tolerzide
Sotazide (Sotalol, hydro-chlorothiazide) Bristol-Myers	1D, 1E	Mild or moderate hypertension	Heart block; bronchospasm; diabetic ketoacidosis; uncontrolled cardiac failure; anaesthesia with myocardial depressant agents; lactation
Spiretic (Spironolactone) DDSA	1E	Aldosterone antagonist (potassium sparing). congestive heart failure; hepatic cirrhosis with ascites and oedema; malignant ascites; nephrotic syndrome; diagnosis and treatment of primary aldosteronism	Acute or significant renal insufficiency, anuria, hyperkalaemia; Addison's disease; hypersensitivity; concurrent potassium sparing diuretics, potassium supplements; pregnancy
Spiroctan (Spironolactone) Boehringer Mannheim	1E	Congestive cardiac failure; cirrhosis with ascites and oedema; malignant ascites; nephrotic syndrome; diagnosis and treatment of primary hyperaldosteronism	Renal failure; acute renal insufficiency; hyperkalaemia; concomitant potassium supplements or potassium sparing drugs/diuretics
Spirotcan-M (Potassium canrenoate) Boehringer Mannheim	1E	Oedema; diagnosis and treatment of primary hyperaldosteronism	Hyperkalaemia; hyponatraemia; severe renal failure; concomitant potassium supplements, potassium sparing drugs/diuretics
Spirolone (Spironolactone) Berk	1E	Congestive heart failure; hepatic cirrhosis with ascites and oedema; malignant ascites and nephrotic syndrome; diagnosis and treatment of hyper-αldosteronism	Renal failure; acute renal insufficiency; hyperkalaemia; concomitant potassium supplements or potassium sparing drugs/diuretics
Spironolactone	1E		Refer to Brand(s): Aldactide, Aldactone, Diatensec, Laractone, Lasilactone, Spiretic, Spiroctan, Spirospare
Spirospare (Spironolactone) Ashbourne	1E	Aldosterone antagonist (potassium sparing). congestive heart failure; hepatic cirrhosis with ascites and oedema; malignant ascites; nephrotic syndrome; diagnosis and treatment of primary aldosteronism	Acute or significant renal insufficiency, anuria, hyperkalaemia; Addison's disease; hypersensitivity; concurrent potassium sparing diuretics, potassium supplements; pregnancy
Stanozolol	1C		Refer to Brand(s): Stromba

THE DOPING DEFINITION OF THE IOC MEDICAL COMMISSION IS BASED ON THE BANNING OF PHARMACEUTICAL CLASSES OF AGENTS.

Adverse Reactions	Comments
Hypotension; bradycardia; cold extremities; headache; dreams; angina; skin rash; dry eyes	Misuse in some sports where physical activity is of little or no importance; the IOC Medical Commission reserves the right to test those sports which it deems are appropriate
Bradycardia; hypotension; cold extremities; angina; sleep disturbances; skin rash; dry eyes; fluid, electrolyte disturbances; gastrointestinal upset; consult literature	Misuse in some sports where physical activity is of little or no importance; the IOC Medical Commission reserves the right to test those sports which it deems are appropriate Deliberate attempts to reduce weight artificially in order to compete in lower weight classes or to dilute urine constitute clear manipulations which are unacceptable on ethical grounds
Breast enlargement (usually reversible); fluid/electrolyte disturbances; gastrointestinal symptoms incl. cramping and diarrhoea; drowsiness; lethargy; headache; mental confusion, ataxia; skin reactions; endocrine disturbances	Deliberate attempts to reduce weight artificially in order to compete in lower weight classes or to dilute urine constitute clear manipulations which are unacceptable on ethical grounds
Drowsiness; mental confusion; gastrointestinal effects; impaired alertness; breast enlargement (usually reversible); skin rash	Deliberate attempts to reduce weight artificially in order to compete in lower weight classes or to dilute urine constitute clear manipulations which are unacceptable on ethical grounds
Irritation at inj. site; transient confusion; nausea, vomiting; hyperkalaemia; consult literature	Deliberate attempts to reduce weight artificially in order to compete in lower weight classes or to dilute urine constitute clear manipulations which are unacceptable on ethical grounds
Breast enlargement (reversible); gastrointestinal effects; drowsiness; mental confusion; headache; skin rashes; menstrual irregularities; impotence	Deliberate attempts to reduce weight artificially in order to compete in lower weight classes or to dilute urine constitute clear manipulations which are unacceptable on ethical grounds
Breast enlargement (usually reversible); fluid/electrolyte disturbances; gastrointestinal symptoms incl. cramping and diarrhoea; drowsiness; lethargy; headache; mental confusion, ataxia; skin reactions; endocrine disturbances	Deliberate attempts to reduce weight artificially in order to compete in lower weight classes or to dilute urine constitute clear manipulations which are unacceptable on ethical grounds

ANY RELATED COMPOUND TO THE EXAMPLES LISTED ABOVE ARE ALSO BANNED.

Brand (Generic) Manufacturer	IOC Category	Indications	Contraindications
Stromba (Stanozolol) Sterling Winthrop	1C	Vascular manifestations of Behcet's disease; prevention of spontaneous attacks of proven hereditary angio-oedema	Not for use as a treatment of weightloss or failure to thrive in children; pregnancy, lactation; established hepatic disease; prostate cancer; porphyria
Sublimaze (Fentanyl) Janssen	1B	Analgesia in anaesthesia	Respiratory depression; obstructive airways disease; concomitant use or within 2 weeks of MAOIs
Sudafed, Sudafed SA (Pseudoephedrine) Wellcome	1A	Upper respiratory tract decongestant	Severe hypertension; severe coronary artery disease; MAOIs (concomitant or within 14 days)
Sudafed Co (Pseudoephedrine, paracetamol) Wellcome	1A	Upper respiratory tract congestion with assoc. or pain	Severe hypertension; severe coronary artery disease; MAOIs (concomitant or within 14 days)
Sudafed Expectorant (Pseudoephedrine, guaiphenesin) Wellcome	1A	Conditions where an expectorant and upper respiratory tract decongestant are required	Severe hypertension; severe coronary artery disease; MAOIs (concomitant or within 14 days); urinary retention in males with prostatic enlargement
Sudafed Linctus (Pseudoephedrine, dextromethorphan) Wellcome	1A	Relief of unproductive cough with congestion	Severe hypertension; severe coronary artery disease; cough assoc. with asthma; MAOIs (concomitant or within 14 days)
Sudafed Plus (Pseudoephedrine, triprolidine) Wellcome	1A	Symptomatic releif of allergic rhinitis	Severe hypertension; severe coronary artery disease; MAOIs (concomitant or within 14 days)
Sustanon 100, Sustanon 250 (Testosterone) Organon	1C	Testosterone replacement therapy in male hypogonadal disorders incl. after castration, eunuchoidism, hypopituitarism, endocrine impotence; male climacteric symptoms, eg. decreased libido; certain types of infertility due to disorders of spermatogenesis; osteoporosis due to androgen deficiency	Known or suspected prostatic or mammary carcinoma
Synacthen (Tetracosactrin) Ciba	1F	Diagnostic test for the investigation of adrenocortical insufficiency	Allergic disorders

THE DOPING DEFINITION OF THE IOC MEDICAL COMMISSION IS BASED ON THE BANNING OF PHARMACEUTICAL CLASSES OF AGENTS.

Adverse Reactions	Comments
Acne; hirsutism; amenorrhoea; voice change; headache; muscle cramp; dyspepsia; skin rash; hair loss; euphoria; depression; cholestatic jaundice	Misused in sport not only to attempt to increase muscle bulk, strength and power when used with increased food intake but also in lower doses and normal food intake to attempt to improve competitiveness
Dependence; complex, consult product literature	Pain of the severity to necessitate narcotic analgesia (with the risk of drug dependence), should prevent sports participation
Insomnia; sleep disturbances; hallucinations; urinary retention in males with prostatic enlargement	
Insomnia; sleep disturbances; hallucinations; possible blood dyscrasias; urinary retention in males with prostatic enlargement	
Insomnia; sleep disturbances; hallucinations; urinary retention in males with prostatic enlargement	
Insomnia, sleep disturbances; hallucinations; urinary retention in males with prostatic enlargement; dizziness; nausea, vomiting, gastrointestinal disturbances	
Insomnia; sleep disturbances; hallucinations; drowsiness; urinary retention in males with prostatic enlargement	
Psychological changes incl. euphoria, depression, psychosis; salt, water retention; gynaecomastia, testicular atrophy, decreased spermatogenesis; changes in libido, prostatic hypertrophy, decreased FSH and LH level; acne, alopecia; tendon ruptures; increased LDL cholesterol, decreased HDL cholesterol; hypertension, atherogenesis, sudden death; kidney tumours; increased transaminases, cholestatic jaundice, peliosis hepatitis; hepatoma, carcinoma of the liver In children: premature epiphyseal closure; premature virilisation	Misused in sport, not only to attempt to increase muscle bulk, strength and power when used with increased food intake but also in lower doses and normal food intake to attempt to improve competitiveness The definition of a positive result is: a ratio in urine of testosterone/epitestosterone >6
Hypersensitivity reactions; consult literature	

ANY RELATED COMPOUND TO THE EXAMPLES LISTED ABOVE ARE ALSO BANNED.

Brand (Generic) Manufacturer	IOC Category	Indications	Contraindications
Synacthen Depot (Tetracosactrin) *Ciba*	1F	Short-term therapy: ulcerative colitis, Crohn's disease, juvenile rheumatoid arthritis; adjunct in rheumatoid arthritis, osteoarthritis; diagnostic aid for investigation of adrenocortical insufficiency	Acute psychoses; infections; peptic ulcer; Cushing's syndrome; refractory heart failure; adrenogenital syndrome; therapeutic use of adrenocortical insufficiency, treatment of asthma or allergic disorders; neonates; intravenous use
Syndol (Codeine, *caffeine*, paracetamol, doxylamine) *Merrell Dow*	1B	Moderate to severe pain	
T&R Gee's Linctus (Opium) *Thornton & Ross*	1B	Cough	
Temgesic (Buprenorphine) *Reckitt & Colman*	1B	Strong analgesic for relief of moderate to severe pain	
Tenif (Atenolol, nifedipine) *Stuart*	1D	Hypertension	2nd or 3rd degree heart block; cardiogenic shock; overt heart failure; concomitant cardiodepressant drugs; women of childbearing potential; lactation
Tenoret 50 (Atenolol, chlorthalidone) *Stuart*	1D, 1E	Management of hypertension	2nd or 3rd degree heart block; cardiogenic shock
Tenoretic (Atenolol, chlorthalidone) *Stuart*	1D, 1E		Refer: Tenoret
Tenormin (Atenolol) *Stuart*	1D	Cardioselective β_1-blocker. Hypertension; angina pectoris; cardiac dysrhythmias; early intervention in the acute phase of myocardial infarction	2nd or 3rd degree heart block; cardiogenic shock
Tenuate Dospan (Diethylpropion) *Merrell Dow*	1A	Anorectic agent for short-term use under supervision for treatment of some patients with moderate or severe obesity	Uncontrolled thyrotoxicosis; emotionally unstable patients; moderate/severe hypertension; severe cardiovascular disease; history of drug abuse; MAOIs (concomitant or within 14 days)

THE DOPING DEFINITION OF THE IOC MEDICAL COMMISSION IS BASED ON THE BANNING OF PHARMACEUTICAL CLASSES OF AGENTS.

Adverse Reactions	Comments
Hypersensitivity reactions; side effects assoc. with excessive adrenocorticotrophic activity; consult literature	
Drowsiness; rash; fever; nightmares; constipation	
	Cough and cold preparations which contain drugs of the narcotic analgesic class are banned
Respiratory depression; drowsiness; nausea, vomiting; dependence	Pain of the severity to necessitate narcotic analgesia (with the risk of drug dependence), should prevent sports participation
Headache; flushing; fatigue; dizziness; oedema; skin rash; dry eyes	Use in some sports where physical activity is of little or no importance; the IOC Medical Commission reserves the right to test those sports which it deems are appropriate
Hypotension; bradycardia; cold extremities; sleep disturbances; muscular fatigue; nausea; skin rash; dry eyes; dizziness; blood dyscrasias	Misuse in some sports where physical activity is of little or no importance; the IOC Medical Commission reserves the right to test those sports which it deems are appropriate Deliberate attempts to reduce weight artificially in order to compete in lower weight classes or to dilute urine constitute clear manipulations which are unacceptable on ethical grounds
Hypotension; bradycardia; cold extremities; headache; muscular fatigue; sleep disturbances; skin rash; dry eyes	Misuse in some sports where physical activity is of little or no importance; the IOC Medical Commission reserves the right to test those sports which it deems are appropriate
Palpitations; tachycardia; elevation of blood pressure; nervousness; agitation; restlessness; insomnia; euphoria; depression; dry mouth; psychoses; hallucinations; dependence; nausea, vomiting; impaired alertness; constipation; rash	

ANY RELATED COMPOUND TO THE EXAMPLES LISTED ABOVE ARE ALSO BANNED.

Brand (Generic) Manufacturer	IOC Category	Indications	Contraindications
Teoptic **(Cartelol)** *Dispersa*	1D	Ocular hypertension; chronic open angle glaucoma	Cardiac insufficiency (uncontrolled); bronchospasm; pregnancy
Terbutaline	1A		Refer to Brand(s): Bricanyl, Bricanyl Expectorant, Bricanyl SA, Monovent
Tercoda **(Codeine,** eucalyptol, terpin, menthol, peppermint oil, pumilio pine oil) *Sinclair*	1B	Chronic and subacute bronchitis	
Teronac **(Mazindol)** *Sandoz*	1A	Aid in establishment of a diet in the treatment of obesity (under supervision)	Peptic ulcer; glaucoma; severe renal, hepatic or cardiac insufficiency; cardiac arrhythmias; severe hypertension; history of psychiatric illness, emotional instability; lactation; MAOIs, adrenergic neurone blockers (concomitant or within 1 month)
Terpoin **(Codeine,** cineole, menthol) *Hough, Hoseason*	1B	Unproductive cough	Hepatic disease
Testosterone	1C		Refer to Brand(s): Primoteston Depot, Prowess, Restandol, Sustanon 100, Sustanon 250, Testosterone Implants, Virormone
Testosterone **Implants** **(Testosterone)** *Organon*	1C	Testosterone replacement therapy in male hypogonadal disorders incl. after castration, eunuchoidism, hypopituitarism, endocrine impotence; male climacteric symptoms, eg. decreased libido; certain types of infertility due to disorders of spermatogenesis; osteoporosis due to androgen deficiency	Known or suspected prostatic or mammary carcinoma
Tetracosactrin	1F		Refer to Brand(s): Synacthen, Synacthen Depot
Thalamonal **(Fentanyl,** droperidol) *Janssen*	1B	Neuroleptanalgesia; premedication; intractable labyrinthine vertigo (eg. Meniere's disease)	Severe depression; obstructive airways disease; respiratory depression (unless ventilating); MAOIs (concomitant or within 14 days)
Timolol	1D		Refer to Brand(s): Betim, Blocadren, Moducren, Prestim, Timoptol

THE DOPING DEFINITION OF THE IOC MEDICAL COMMISSION IS BASED ON THE BANNING OF PHARMACEUTICAL CLASSES OF AGENTS.

Adverse Reactions	Comments
Local ocular reactions; bradycardia; dyspnoea; headache; lassitude; vertigo	Misuse in some sport where physical activity is of little or no importance; the IOC Medical Commission reserves the right to test those sports which it deems are appropriate
Constipation	Cough and cold preparations which contain drugs of the narcotic analgesic class are banned
Constipation; sweating; dry mouth; insomnia; nervousness; headache; syncope; dizziness; chills; skin rash; disturbances of micturition, sexual function (reversible); tachycardia; euphoria; hallucinations; impaired alertness; dependence	
Constipation	Cough and cold preparations which contain drugs of the narcotic analgesic class are banned
Psychological changes incl. euphoria, depression, psychosis; salt, water retention; gynaecomastia, testicular atrophy, decreased spermatogenesis; changes in libido, prostatic hypertrophy, decreased FSH and LH level; acne, alopecia; tendon ruptures; increased LDL cholesterol, decreased HDL cholesterol; hypertension, atherogenesis, sudden death; kidney tumours; increased transaminases, cholestatic jaundice, peliosis hepatitis; hepatoma, carcinoma of the liver In children: premature epiphyseal closure; premature virilisation	Misused in sport, not only to attempt to increase muscle bulk, strength and power when used with increased food intake but also in lower doses and normal food intake to attempt to improve competitiveness The definition of a positive result is: a ratio in urine of testosterone/epitestosterone >6
Tolerance, dependence; respiratory depression; impaired alertness	Pain of the severity to necessitate narcotic analgesia (with the risk of drug dependence), should prevent sports participation

ANY RELATED COMPOUND TO THE EXAMPLES LISTED ABOVE ARE ALSO BANNED.

Brand (Generic) Manufacturer	IOC Category	Indications	Contraindications
Timoptol (Timolol) *Merck Sharp & Dohme*	1D	Reduction of elevated intraocular pressure; open angle glaucoma	Bronchospasm, incl. bronchial asthma, or severe chronic obstructive pulmonary disease; sinus bradycardia, 2nd and 3rd degree heart block, overt cardiac failure, cardiogenic shock
Tolerzide (Sotalol, hydro-chlorothiazide) *Bristol-Myers*	1D, 1E	Mild to moderate hypertension	Heart block; bronchospasm; diabetic ketoacidosis; impending or uncontrolled cardiac failure; myocardial depressant anaesthetics; lactation
Totamol (Atenolol) *CP Pharmaceuticals*	1D	Management of hypertension; angina pectoris; cardiac dysrhythmias; early intervention in the acute phase of myocardial infarction	Severe bradycardia; 2nd or 3rd degree heart block; heart failure; intermittent claudication
Trandate (Labetalol) *Duncan Flockhart*	1D	Treatment of all grades of hypertension; angina pectoris with existing hypertension; IV: rapid control of blood pressure, hypertensive episodes following acute myocardial infarction	2nd or 3rd degree heart block; cardiogenic shock; other conditions assoc. with severe and prolonged hypotension or severe bradycardia
Trasicor (Oxprenolol) *Ciba*	1D	Angina pectoris; hypertension; cardiac arrhythmias; short-term relief of somatic symptoms of anxiety; other cardiovascular indications, consult literature	2nd or 3rd degree heart block; marked bradycardia; uncontrolled heart failure; cardiogenic shock; sick-sinus syndrome; bronchial asthma; anaesthesia with ether, chloroform
Trasidrex (Oxprenolol, cyclopenthiazide) *Ciba*	1D, 1E	Mild and moderate hypertension	2nd or 3rd degree heart block; marked bradycardia; uncontrolled heart failure; cardiogenic shock; marked renal insufficiency; concomitant lithium
Triamcinolone	3D		Refer to Brand(s): Kenalog, Ledercort
Triamco (Hydrochloro-thiazide, triamterene) *Norton*	1E	Potassium sparing diuretic. Treatment of oedema; mild to moderate hypertension	Other potassium sparing agents; progressive renal disease; hyperkalaemia; pregnancy; lactation
Triamterene	1E		Refer to Brand(s): Dyazide, Dytac, Dytide, Frusene, Kalspare, Triamco

THE DOPING DEFINITION OF THE IOC MEDICAL COMMISSION IS BASED ON THE BANNING OF PHARMACEUTICAL CLASSES OF AGENTS.

Adverse Reactions	Comments
Ocular irritation; bradycardia; arrhythmia; hypotension; syncope; heart block; cerebrovascular accident; cerebral ischaemia; congestive heart failure; palpitation; cardiac arrest; bronchospasm; respiratory failure; dyspnoea; headache; asthenia; nausea; dizziness; depression; hypersensitivity reactions	Misuse in some sports where physical activity is of little or no importance; the IOC Medical Commission reserves the right to test those sports which it deems are appropriate
Dyspnoea; tiredness, dizziness, lightheadedness; headache; fever; excessive bradycardia; skin rash; dry eyes; hyperuricaemia; photosensitivity	Misuse in some sports where physical activity is of little or no importance; the IOC Medical Commission reserves the right to test those sports which it deems are appropriate Deliberate attempts to reduce weight artificially in order to compete in lower weight classes or to dilute urine constitute clear manipulations which are unacceptable on ethical grounds
Bradycardia; hypotension; cold extremities; sleep disturbances; muscular fatigue; skin rash; dry eyes	Misuse in some sports where physical activity is of little or no importance; the IOC Medical Commission reserves the right to test those sports which it deems are appropriate
Hypotension; bradycardia; cold extremities; headache; tiredness; depression; dizziness; lethargy; nasal congestion; sweating; tremor; difficult micturition; epigastric pain; nausea, vomiting; consult literature	Misuse in some sports where physical activity is of little or no importance; the IOC Medical Commission reserves the right to test those sports which it deems are appropriate
Hypotension; bradycardia; cold extremities; headache; sleep disturbances; dizziness, drowsiness; insomnia; excitement; dry mouth; vision disturbances; keratoconjunctivitis; loss of libido; gastrointestinal disturbances; bronchospasm; dyspnoea; heart failure	Misuse in some sports where physical activity is of little or no importance; the IOC Medical Commission reserves the right to test those sports which it deems are appropriate
Dizziness; drowsiness; headache; insomnia; excitement; gastro-intestinal disturbances; bradycardia; thrombocytopenia; bronchospasm; heart failure; cold extremities; skin rash; dry eyes; precipitation of latent gout, latent diabetes; skin rash	Misuse in some sports where physical activity is of little or no importance; the IOC Medical Commission reserves the right to test those sports which it deems are appropriate Deliberate attempts to reduce weight artificially in order to compete in lower weight classes or to dilute urine constitute clear manipulations which are unacceptable on ethical grounds
Muscle cramps; weakness; dizziness; headache; dry mouth; anaphylaxis; rash; urticaria; photosensitivity and purpura; nausea; vomiting; diarrhoea; constipation	Deliberate attempts to reduce weight artificially in order to compete in lower weight classes or to dilute urine constitute clear manipulations which are unacceptable on ethical grounds

ANY RELATED COMPOUND TO THE EXAMPLES LISTED ABOVE ARE ALSO BANNED.

Brand (Generic) Manufacturer	IOC Category	Indications	Contraindications
Triogesic (**Phenylpropanol-amine**, paracetamol) *Intercare*	1A	Nasal, sinus congestion and assoc. pain	
Triominic (**Phenylpropanol-amine**, pheniramine) *Intercare*	1A	Nasal congestion; allergic rhinitis; hayfever	
Tylex (**Codeine**, paracetamol) *Cilag*	1B	Pain (severe)	
Uniflu (**Codeine**, *caffeine*, paracetamol, diphenhydramine, **phenylephrine**) *Unigreg*	1B	Colds and flu	Cardiovascular disorders; hyperthyroidism; hepatic disease; concomitant CNS depressants incl. alcohol
Urine Substitution/ Tampering	2B		
Vasaten (**Atenolol**)	1D	Cardioselective β_1-blocker. Hypertension; angina pectoris; cardiac dysrhythmias; early intervention in the acute phase of myocardial infarction	2nd or 3rd degree heart block; cardiogenic shock
Vasetic (**Amiloride, hydro-chlorothiazide**) *Shire*	1E	Potassium sparing diuretic. Hypertension; congestive heart failure; hepatic cirrhosis with ascites	Hyperkalaemia; concomitant potassium supplements or potassium sparing drugs/ diuretics; anuria, acute renal failure, severe progressive renal disease; severe hepatic failure; hepatic precoma; Addison's disease; hypercalcaemia; concurrent lithium; diabetic nephropathy; hyperuricaemia; diabetes mellitus
Vasoxine (**Methoxamine**) *Wellcome*	1A	Counteraction of hypotension	Pre-existent severe hypertension
Veganin (**Codeine**, aspirin, paracetamol) *Warner-Lambert*	1B	Analgesic	Stomach ulcer

THE DOPING DEFINITION OF THE IOC MEDICAL COMMISSION IS BASED ON THE BANNING OF PHARMACEUTICAL CLASSES OF AGENTS.

Adverse Reactions	Comments
Lightheadedness; dizziness; sedation; shortness of breath; nausea, vomiting; allergic reaction; euphoria; dysphoria; constipation, abdominal pain; pruritus; dependence	Pain of the severity to necessitate narcotic analgesia should prevent sports participation
Drowsiness; tachycardia; arrhythmias; dry mouth; CNS stimulation, constipation	Cough and cold preparations which contain drugs of the narcotic analgesic and stimulant classes are banned
	Substances and methods which alter the integrity of urine samples used in doping controls are banned
Hypotension; bradycardia; cold extremities; headache; muscular fatigue; sleep disturbances; skin rash; dry eyes	Misuse in some sports where physical activity is of little or no importance; the IOC Medical Commission reserves the right to test those sports which it deems are appropriate
Anorexia, nausea, vomiting, abdominal fullness, gastric irritation, cramping, pain, constipation, diarrhoea; dry mouth and thirst; paraesthesias; transient blurred vision; inflammation of a salivary gland; dizziness, vertigo, weakness, fatigability; muscle cramps; orthostatic hypotension; skin rash, pruritus; minor psychiatric disturbances; transient visual disturbances; haematological disturbances; purpura; rash; vasculitis; fever; respiratory distress; headache; restlessness; jaundice; pancreatitis; xanthopsia; hyperglycaemia; glycosuria; hyperuricaemia	Deliberate attempts to reduce weight artificially in order to compete in lower weight classes or to dilute urine constitute clear manipulations which are unacceptable on ethical grounds
Complex, consult literature	

ANY RELATED COMPOUND TO THE EXAMPLES LISTED ABOVE ARE ALSO BANNED.

Brand (Generic) Manufacturer	IOC Category	Indications	Contraindications
Ventolin Tablets, Syrup, Injection (Salbutamol) *Allen & Hanburys*	1A	Relief of bronchospasm in asthma, chronic bronchitis, emphysema	
Ventolin Infusion (Salbutamol) *Allen & Hanburys*	1A	Prevention of premature labour; bronchospasm	Threatened abortion during 1st or 2nd trimester of pregnancy
Vibrocil (Phenylephrine, dimethindene, neomycin) *Zyma*	1A	Common cold, acute sinusitis, rhinitis, complicated by Staphylococcal infections	Cardiovascular disease; thyrotoxicosis; closed angle glaucoma; children <2 years; pregnancy, lactation; MAOIs (concomitant or within 14 days)
Vicks Cold Care (Paracetamol, dextromethorphan, **phenylpropanolamine**) *Procter & Gamble*	1A	Colds	
Vicks Medinite (**Ephedrine**, dextromethorphan, doxylamine, paracetamol, alcohol) *Procter & Gamble*	1A	Colds (night-time)	
Villescon (**Prolintane**, vitamins) *Boehringer Ingelheim*	1A	Tonic after illness, surgery, labour; apathy and anorexia in elderly; institutional neuroses; anorexia, lassitude following radiotherapy	Thyrotoxicosis; epilepsy
Virormone (Testosterone) *Paines & Byrne*	1C	Testosterone replacement in castrated males; hypogonadism due to pituitary or testicular disease; also control of breast carcinoma in post-menopausal women	Breast or prostatic carcinoma in males; nephrosis; closed epiphyses; pregnancy, lactation
Viskaldix (**Pindolol, clopamide**) *Sandoz*	1D, 1E	Mild to moderate hypertension	Cardiac failure (unless controlled); heart block; pronounced bradycardia; obstructive pulmonary disease; cor pulmonale; severe renal or hepatic failure; metabolic acidosis; prolonged fasting; hypokalaemia; concomitant calcium channel blockers, lithium; pregnancy, lactation

THE DOPING DEFINITION OF THE IOC MEDICAL COMMISSION IS BASED ON THE BANNING OF PHARMACEUTICAL CLASSES OF AGENTS.

Adverse Reactions	Comments
Fine tremor of skeletal muscle; increases in heart rate; headaches; nausea; palpitations; sensations of warmth	Salbutamol via inhalation only is permitted; oral and injectable forms are banned
Tremor; high doses can cause peripheral vasodilation; increased heart rate; transient muscle cramps; hypersensitivity reactions; nausea, vomiting; headaches	Salbutamol via inhalation only is permitted; oral and injectable forms are banned
Transient local reactions; rebound congestion	
Tachycardia; nausea; colicky abdominal pain; sleeplessness	
Consult literature	Misused in sport, not only to attempt to increase muscle bulk, strength and power when used with increased food intake but also in lower doses and normal food intake to attempt to improve competitiveness The definition of a positive result is: a ratio in urine of testosterone/epitestosterone >6
Hypotension; headaches; depression; diarrhoea; insomnia; sleep disturbances; epigastric pain; fatigue; dizziness; skin rash; dry eyes	Misuse in some sports where physical activity is of little or no importance; the IOC Medical Commission reserves the right to test those sports which it deems are appropriate Deliberate attempts to reduce weight artificially in order to compete in lower weight classes or to dilute urine constitute clear manipulations which are unacceptable on ethical grounds

ANY RELATED COMPOUND TO THE EXAMPLES LISTED ABOVE ARE ALSO BANNED.

Brand (Generic) Manufacturer	IOC Category	Indications	Contraindications
Visken **(Pindolol)** *Sandoz*	1D	Hypertension; angina pectoris	Cardiac failure (unless controlled); heart block; pronounced bradycardia; obstructive pulmonary disease; cor pulmonale; metabolic acidosis; prolonged fasting; severe renal failure; concomitant calcium channel blockers; pregnancy, lactation
Volital **(Pemoline)** *Laboratories for Applied Biology*	1A	Hyperkinetic syndrome in children >6 years	Glaucoma; extrapyramidal disorders; hyperexcitable states (thyrotoxicosis)
Volmax **(Salbutamol)** *Duncan Flockhart*	1A	Relief of bronchospasm in asthma, chronic bronchitis, emphysema	
Wig Gee's **(Opium)**	1B	Cough	
Xamoterol	1A		Refer to Brand(s): Corwin
Xipamide	1A		Refer to Brand(s): Diurexan
Xylocaine with **Adrenaline** **(Adrenaline,** lignocaine) *Astra*	3C	Local or regional anaesthesia	Anaesthesia of fingers, toes, tip of nose, ears, penis; IV admin
Yutopar **(Ritodrine)** *Duphar*	1A	Management of uncomplicated preterm labour; fetal asphyxia in labour	Antepartum haemorrhage demanding immed. delivery; eclampsia, severe pre-eclampsia; intra-uterine fetal death; chorioamnionitis; maternal cardiac disease; cord compression

THE DOPING DEFINITION OF THE IOC MEDICAL COMMISSION IS BASED ON THE BANNING OF PHARMACEUTICAL CLASSES OF AGENTS.

Adverse Reactions	Comments
Depression; diarrhoea; insomnia; headaches; sleep disturbances; epigastric pain; fatigue; dizziness; hypotension; consult literature	Misuse in some sports where physical activity is of little or no importance; the IOC Medical Commission reserves the right to test those sports which it deems are appropriate
Mouth dryness; abdominal pain; sweating; palpitations; nausea; headache; irritability; excitability; night terrors; anorexia; insomnia Complex, consult literature	
Fine tremor of skeletal muscle; increases in heart rate; headaches; nausea; palpitations; sensations of warmth	Salbutamol via inhalation only is permitted; oral and injectable forms are banned
	Cough and cold preparations which contain drugs of the narcotic analgesic class are banned
Inadvertent subarachnoid injection may lead to cardiovascular collapse, CNS depression, respiratory arrest More common reactions incl. nervousness, dizziness, blurred vision, tremor, drowsiness, tinnitus, numbness, disorientation, nausea, vomiting; see product literature	
Increased maternal pulse rate; tachycardia, palpitation, flushing; sweating; tremor; nausea, vomiting	

ANY RELATED COMPOUND TO THE EXAMPLES LISTED ABOVE ARE ALSO BANNED.

Permitted Products

Permitted Products

This list is not exhaustive, nor is it intended to be, as there are other preparations which do not contain banned drugs. Further information is available from: Doping Control Unit, The Sports Council
Walken House, 3-10 Melton Street
London NW1 2EB
Tel: 071-383-5411, 071-383-5667

Index

PoM = Prescription-only Medicines

1. Alimentary System

(a) Hyperacidity, reflux and ulcers

Actal Tablets *(Sterling Health)*
Actonorm Gel, Powder *(Wallace)*
Algicon *(Rorer)*
PoM Algitec *(SK&F)*
PoM Alimix *(Cilag)*
Alka-Donna *(Carlton)*
Alka-Seltzer *(Bayer)*
Almasilate Suspension *(Unbranded)*
Altacite Plus *(Roussel)*
Alu-Cap *(3M Health Care)*
Aludrox *(Charwell)*
Aluhyde *(Sinclair)*
Aluminium Hydroxide Tabs/Mixt. *(Unbranded)*
Alvercol *(Norgine)*
Andrews Answer [NB. Contains caffeine] *(Sterling Health)*
Andrews Liver Salts *(Sterling Health)*
Andursil *(Ciba)*
PoM Antepsin *(Wyeth)*
PoM APP *(Consolidated)*
Asilone *(Boots)*
PoM Axid *(Lilly)*
Bellocarb *(Sinclair)*
PoM Biogastrone *(Sterling Winthrop)*
Birley Antacid Powder *(Torbet)*
Bismag *(Whitehall)*
Bisma Rex *(3M Health Care)*
Bisodol *(Whitehall)*
Buscopan *(Boehringer Ing.)*
PoM Cantil *(BM Pharm)*
Carbellon *(Torbet)*
Caved-S *(Tillotts)*
PoM Colofac *(Duphar)*
Colpermin *(Tillotts)*
PoM Colven *(Reckitt & Colman)*
PoM Cytotec *(Searle)*
De-Nol *(Brocades)*
De-Noltab *(Brocades)*
De Witt's Antacid Powder, Tablets *(De Witt)*
Dijex *(Crookes)*
Diovol *(Pharmax)*
PoM Duogastrone *(Sterling Winthrop)*
Dynese *(Galen)*
PoM Dyspamet *(Bridge)*
Eno *(SmithKline Beecham)*
Gastrils *(Jackson)*
PoM Gastrobid Continus *(Napp)*
Gastrocote *(BM Pharm)*
PoM Gastroflux *(Ashbourne)*
PoM Gastromax *(Farmitalia)*
Gastron *(Sterling Winthrop)*
PoM Gastrozepin *(Boots)*
Gaviscon *(Reckitt & Colman)*
Gelusil *(Warner-Lambert)*

Hydrotalcite Susp. *(Unbranded)*
Kolanticon *(Merrell Dow)*
PoM Losec *(Astra)*
Maalox, Maalox Plus *(Rhone-Poulenc)*
Maclean Indigestion Tablets *(SmithKline Beecham)*
Magaldrate Suspension *(Unbranded)*
Magnesium Trisilicate Mixt. *(Unbranded)*
Malinal *(Wyeth)*
PoM Maxolon *(Beecham)*
PoM Merbentyl *(Merrell Dow)*
PoM Metox *(Steinhard)*
Milk of Magnesia Liquid, Tablets *(Sterling Health)*
Mintec *(Innovex)*
Moorland Tablets *(Crookes)*
PoM Mucaine *(Wyeth)*
Mucogel *(Pharmax)*
PoM Nacton, Nacton Forte *(Bencard)*
Novasil *(Cupal)*
Nulacin *(Bencard)*
Opas *(Leo)*
PoM Parmid *(Lagap)*
PoM Pepcid PM *(Morson)*
Pepto-Bismol *(Proctor & Gamble)*
PoM Piptal *(BM Pharm)*
PoM Piptalin *(BM Pharm)*
Polyalk Revised Formula *(Galen)*
Polycrol, Polycrol Forte *(Nicholas)*
Premiums Antacid Tablets *(Newton)*
PoM Prepulsid *(Janssen)*
PoM Primperan *(Berk)*
PoM Pro-Banthine *(Gold Cross)*
PoM Pyrogastrone *(Sterling Winthrop)*
Rennie *(Nicholas)*
Resolve *(SmithKline Beecham)*
Roter *(Roterpharma)*
Setlers *(SmithKline Beecham)*
Setlers Tums *(SmithKline Beecham)*
Siloxyl *(Martindale)*
Simeco *(Wyeth)*
Sodium Bicarb. Tabs. Co. *(Unbranded)*
Sovol *(Carter-Wallace)*
Spasmonal *(Norgine)*
PoM Tagamet *(SK&F)*
Topal *(ICI)*
Unigest *(Unigreg)*
Windcheaters *(Napp)*
PoM Zantac *(Glaxo)*

(b) Laxatives

Agarol *(Warner-Lambert)*
Alophen *(Warner-Lambert)*
Bisacodyl *(Unbranded)*

Carbalax *(Pharmax)*
Celevac *(Boehringer Ing.)*
PoM Co-Danthromer *(Unbranded)*
PoM Co-Danthrusate *(Unbranded)*
PoM Codalax *(Napp)*
Cologel *(Lilly)*
Dioctyl *(Medo)*
Dulcolax *(Boehringer Ing.)*
Duphalac *(Duphar)*
Fletchers' Arachis Oil *(Pharmax)*
Fletchers' Enemette *(Pharmax)*
Fletchers' Phosphate *(Pharmax)*
Fybogel *(Reckitt & Colman)*
Fybranta *(Norgine)*
Glycerol Suppositories *(Unbranded)*
PoM GoLytely *(Seward)*
Isogel *(Allen & Hanburys)*
Kest *(Torbet)*
Klean-Prep *(Norgine)*
Lactulose Solution *(Unbranded)*
Laxoberal *(Windsor)*
Lejfibre *(Britannia)*
Magnesium Sulph. Mixt. *(Unbranded)*
Manevac *(Galen)*
PoM Mestinon *(Roche)*
Metamucil *(Procter & Gamble)*
Micolette *(Cusi)*
Micralax *(Evans)*
Milk of Magnesia *(Sterling Health)*
Mil-par *(Sterling Health)*
PoM Myotonine *(Glenwood)*
Normacol *(Norgine)*
PoM Normax *(Evans)*
Nylax *(Crookes)*
Petrolagar *(Whitehall)*
Picolax *(Nordic)*
Proctofibe *(Roussel)*
PoM Prostigmin *(Roche)*
Regulan *(Procter & Gamble)*
Regulettes *(Cupal)*
Relaxit *(Pharmacia)*
Senlax *(Intercare)*
Senna Tablets *(Unbranded)*
Senokot *(Reckitt & Colman)*
Sodium Picosulphate *(Unbranded)*
Trifyba *(Sanofi)*
PoM Ubretid *(Rorer)*
Veripaque *(Sterling Research)*
X-Prep *(Napp)*

(c) Antidiarrhoeals

Beware, some antidiarrhoeals may contain codeine

Arret *(Janssen)*
Celevac *(Boehringer Ing.)*
PoM Deseril *(Sandoz)*
Dioralyte *(Rorer)*
Electrolade *(Nicholas)*
Gluco-Lyte *(Cupal)*

PoM Guarem *(Rybar)*
PoM Imodium *(Janssen)*
KLN *(Nicholas)*
Kao-C *(Cupal)*
Kaopectate *(Upjohn)*
PoM Lomotil *(Gold Cross)*
PoM Questran A *(Bristol-Myers)*
Rehidrat *(Searle)*

(d) Acids, digestive enzymes, cholagogues, cholelitholytics

PoM Chendol Tablets *(CP Pharm)*
PoM Chenofalk *(Thames)*
Cotazym *(Organon)*
Creon *(Duphar)*
PoM Destolit *(Merrell Dow)*
Muripsin *(Norgine)*
Nutrizym GR *(Merck)*
Pancrease *(Cilag)*
Pancrex Granules *(Paines & Byrne)*
Pancrex V Capsules, Powder, Tablets *(Paines & Byrne)*
Pancrex V Forte Tablets *(Paines & Byrne)*
PoM Rowachol *(Monmouth)*
PoM Ursofalk *(Thames)*

(e) Topical rectal medication

PoM Anacal *(Panpharma)*
PoM Anugesic-HC *(Parke Davis)*
Anusol *(Parke Davis)*
PoM Anusol HC *(Parke Davis)*
PoM Asacol *(SK&F)*
PoM Dipentum *(Pharmacia)*
Lasonil *(Bayer)*
PoM Pentasa *(Nordic)*
PoM Proctofoam HC *(Stafford-Miller)*
PoM Proctosedyl *(Roussel)*
PoM Salazopyrin *(Pharmacia)*
PoM Scheriproct *(Schering HC)*
PoM Ultraproct *(Schering HC)*
PoM Uniroid *(Unigreg)*
PoM Xyloproct *(Astra)*

2. Cardiovascular System

(a) Antihypertensives

PoM Accupro *(Parke Davis)*
PoM Acepril *(DF)*
PoM Adalat Retard *(Bayer)*
PoM Aldomet *(MSD)*
PoM Apresoline *(Ciba)*
PoM Arfonad *(Roche)*
PoM Baratol *(Wyeth)*
PoM Bendogen *(Lagap)*
PoM Calcilat *(Eastern)*
PoM Capoten *(Squibb)*
PoM Carace *(Morson)*
PoM Cardene *(Syntex)*

PoM Cardura *(Invicta)*
PoM Catapres *(Boehringer Ing.)*
PoM Coracten *(Evans)*
PoM Cordilox 160 *(Abbott)*
PoM Coversyl *(Servier)*
PoM Decaserpyl *(Roussel)*
PoM Declinax *(Roche)*
PoM Dibenyline *(SK&F)*
PoM Dopamet *(Berk)*
PoM Esbatal *(Calmic)*
PoM Eudemine *(Allen & Hanburys)*
PoM Hydralazine *(Unbranded)*
PoM Hypercal *(Carlton)*
PoM Hypercal-B [CD] *(Carlton)*
PoM Hypovase *(Invicta)*
PoM Hytrin *(Abbott)*
PoM Innovace *(MSD)*
PoM Ismelin *(Ciba)*
PoM Istin *(Pfizer)*
PoM Loniten *(Upjohn)*
PoM Medomet *(DDSA)*
PoM Methyldopa *(Unbranded)*
PoM Prescal *(Ciba)*
PoM Rogitine *(Ciba)*
PoM Securon SR *(Knoll)*
PoM Serpasil *(Ciba)*
PoM Staril *(Squibb)*
PoM Tritace *(Hoechst)*
PoM Univer *(Rorer)*
PoM Verapamil *(Unbranded)*
PoM Zestril *(ICI)*

(b) Antiarrhythmics, cardiac failure

PoM Accupro *(Parke Davis)*
PoM Acepril *(DF)*
PoM Adalat IC *(Bayer)*
PoM Apresoline *(Ciba)*
PoM Arythmol *(Knoll)*
PoM Berkatens *(Berk)*
PoM Bretylate *(Wellcome)*
PoM Capoten *(Squibb)*
PoM Carace *(Morson)*
PoM Cedilanid *(Sandoz)*
PoM Cedocard *(Tillotts)*
PoM Cordarone X *(Sanofi)*
PoM Cordilox *(Abbott)*
PoM Dirythmin SA *(Astra)*
PoM Elantan *(Schwarz)*
PoM Epanutin Parenteral *(Parke Davis)*
PoM Hypovase *(Invicta)*
PoM Innovace *(MSD)*
PoM Ismo *(BM Pharm)*
PoM Isoket Infusion *(Schwarz)*
Isordil *(Wyeth)*
PoM Isotrate *(Thames)*
PoM Kiditard *(Delandale)*
PoM Kinidin Durules *(Astra)*
PoM Lanoxin *(Wellcome)*
PoM Mexitil *(Boehringer Ing.)*
PoM Min-I-Jet Lignocaine (without Adrenaline) *(IMS)*
PoM Nipride *(Roche)*

PoM Nitrocine *(Schwarz)*
PoM Nitronal *(Lipha)*
PoM Pecram *(Zyma)*
PoM Perfan *(Merrell Dow)*
Phyllocontin *(Napp)*
PoM Primacor *(Sterling Winthrop)*
PoM Procainamide Durules *(Astra)*
PoM Pronestyl *(Squibb)*
PoM Prostin VR *(Upjohn)*
PoM Rythmodan *(Roussel)*
PoM Securon *(Knoll)*
PoM Select-A-Jet Lignocaine *(IMS)*
Suscard Buccal *(Pharmax)*
PoM Tambocor *(3M Health Care)*
PoM Tonocard *(Astra)*
PoM Tridil *(Du Pont)*
PoM Uniphyllin Continus *(Napp)*
PoM Vasad *(Shire)*
Vascardin *(Nicholas)*
PoM Verapamil *(Unbranded)*
PoM Xylocard *(Astra)*
PoM Zestril *(ICI)*

(c) Antianginals

PoM Adalat *(Bayer)*
PoM Adizem, Adizem-SR *(Napp)*
PoM Angiozem *(Ashbourne)*
PoM Britiazim *(Thames)*
PoM Calcilat *(Eastern)*
PoM Cardene *(Syntex)*
Cardiacap *(Consoldiated)*
Cedocard Retard *(Tillotts)*
PoM Coracten *(Evans)*
PoM Cordilox *(Abbott)*
Coro-Nitro *(BM Pharm)*
Deponit *(Schwarz)*
Elantan *(Schwarz)*
Glyceryl Trinitrate *(Unbranded)*
GTN 300 mcg *(Martindale)*
PoM Imdur *(Astra)*
PoM Ismo *(BM Pharm)*
Isoket Retard *(Schwarz)*
Isordil *(Wyeth)*
PoM Isotrate *(Thames)*
PoM Istin *(Pfizer)*
MCR-50 *(Tillotts)*
PoM Monit *(Stuart)*
Mono-Cedocard *(Tillotts)*
Mycardol *(Sterling Winthrop)*
PoM Nifedipine *(Unbranded)*
PoM Nitrocine *(Schwarz)*
Nitrocontin Continus *(Degussa)*
Nitrolingual *(Lipha)*
Percutol *(Cusi)*
PoM Securon *(Knoll)*
Soni-Slo *(Lipha)*
Sorbichew *(Stuart)*
Sorbid SA *(Stuart)*
Sorbitrate *(Stuart)*
Suscard Buccal *(Pharmax)*
Sustac *(Pharmax)*
PoM Tildiem *(Lorex)*
Transiderm-Nitro *(Ciba)*
PoM Univer *(Rorer)*

Vascardin *(Nicholas)*
PoM Verapamil *(Unbranded)*

(d) Beta-blockers

All beta-blockers are banned

(e) Hypolipidaemic agents

PoM Atromid-S *(ICI)*
PoM Bezalip-Mono *(BM Pharm)*
    Bradilan *(Napp)*
PoM Colestid *(Upjohn)*
PoM Lipantil *(Norgine)*
PoM Lipostat *(Squibb)*
PoM Lopid *(Parke Davis)*
PoM Lurselle *(Merrell Dow)*
    Maxepa *(DF)*
PoM Olbetam *(Farmitalia)*
PoM Questran A *(Bristol-Myers)*
PoM Zocor *(MSD)*

(f) Antimigraine preparations

Caution! Some products contain
caffeine. Refer Doping Classes and
Methods, Explanations

PoM Cafergot [NB. Contains
    caffeine] *(Sandoz)*
PoM Deseril *(Sandoz)*
PoM Dihydergot Inj. *(Sandoz)*
PoM Dixarit *(Boehringer Ing.)*
PoM Lingraine *(Sterling Winthrop)*
PoM Medihaler-Ergotamine *(3M
    Health Care)*
PoM Migravess, Migravess Forte
    (Bayer)
PoM Migril [NB. Contains caffeine]
    (Wellcome)
PoM Paramax *(Bencard)*
PoM Sanomigran *(Sandoz)*

(g) Other cardiovascular agents, circulatory disorders

PoM Adalat *(Bayer)*
    Bradilan *(Napp)*
    Cyclobral *(Norgine)*
    Cyclospasmol *(Brocades)*
    Hexopal *(Sterling Winthrop)*
PoM Hydergine *(Sandoz)*
PoM Hypovase *(Invicta)*
PoM Nifedipine *(Unbranded)*
PoM Nimotop *(Bayer)*
PoM Opilon *(Parke Davis)*
PoM Praxilene *(Lipha)*
    Ronicol *(Roche)*
    Stugeron Forte *(Janssen)*
PoM Trental *(Hoechst)*
    Vita-E Gels *(Bioglan)*

3. Blood and Haemopoietic Tissues

(a) Iron and haemopoietic agents

Note. All anabolic and erythropoietic
agents are banned

    BC 500 with Iron *(Wyeth)*
    Fefol Spansule *(SK&F)*
    Fefol Z Spansule *(SK&F)*
    Fefol-Vit Spansule *(SK&F)*
    Feospan Spansule *(SK&F)*
    Feravol *(Carlton)*
PoM Ferfolic SV *(Sinclair)*
    Fergon *(Sterling Winthrop)*
    Ferrocap *(Consolidated)*
    Ferrocontin Continus *(Degussa)*
    Ferrocontin Folic Continus
    (Degussa)
    Ferrograd, Ferrograd C *(Abbott)*
    Ferrograd Folic *(Abbott)*
    Ferromyn *(Wellcome)*
    Ferrous Gluconate *(Unbranded)*
    Ferrous Sulphate *(Unbranded)*
    Fersaday *(DF)*
    Fersamal *(DF)*
    Fesovit Spansule *(SK&F)*
    Fesovit Z Spansule *(SK&F)*
    Folex-350 *(Rybar)*
PoM Folic Acid *(Unbranded)*
PoM Folicin *(Paines & Byrne)*
    Forceval *(Unigreg)*
    Galfer *(Galen)*
    Givitol *(Galen)*
PoM Imferon *(Fisons)*
    Iron Jelloids *(SmithKline
    Beecham)*
    Ironplan *(Wellcome)*
PoM Jectofer *(Astra)*
PoM Lexpec, Lexpec with Iron *(RP
    Drugs)*
PoM Meterfolic *(Sinclair)*
    Niferex *(Tillotts)*
    Phillips Iron Tonic Tablets
    (Phillips Yeast)
    Plesmet *(Napp)*
    Pregaday *(DF)*
    Pregnavite Forte F *(Bencard)*
    Slow-Fe *(Ciba)*
PoM Slow-Fe Folic *(Ciba)*
    Sytron *(Parke Davis)*

(b) Anticoagulants, antithrombotics and fibrinolytics

PoM Actilyse *(Boehringer Ing.)*
    Angettes *(Bristol-Myers)*
PoM Arvin *(Rorer)*
PoM Calciparine *(Sanofi)*
PoM Clexane *(Rhone-Poulenc)*
PoM Dindevan *(DF)*

PoM Eminase *(Beecham)*
PoM Flolan *(Wellcome)*
PoM Fragmin *(Kabi)*
PoM Hep-Flush *(Leo)*
PoM Heplok *(Leo)*
PoM Hepsal *(CP Pharm)*
PoM Kabikinase *(Kabi)*
PoM Marevan *(DF)*
PoM Minihep *(Leo)*
PoM Monoparin *(CP Pharm)*
PoM Multiparin *(CP Pharm)*
    Nu-Seals Aspirin *(Lilly)*
PoM Persantin *(Boehringer Ing.)*
    Platet 300 *(Nicholas)*
PoM Pump-Hep *(Leo)*
PoM Sinthrome *(Geigy)*
PoM Streptase *(Hoechst)*
PoM Ukidan *(Serono)*
PoM Unihep *(Leo)*
PoM Uniparin *(CP Pharm)*
PoM Vasyrol *(Shire)*

(c) Haemostatics

PoM Cyklokapron *(Kabi)*
PoM Dicynene *(Delandale)*
PoM Konakion *(Roche)*
PoM Monoclate-P *(Armour)*
    Synkavit *(Roche)*
PoM Trasylol *(Bayer)*

4. Central Nervous System

(a) Analgesics, antipyretics

Combination analgesics may contain
drugs of the banned narcotic class eg.
codeine; check carefully. Some
products may also contain caffeine,
refer Explanations of Doping Classes
and Methods

    Actron [NB. Contains caffeine]
    (Bayer)
PoM Acupan *(3M Health Care)*
    Anadin Ibuprofen *(Whitehall)*
    Anadin Paracetamol *(Whitehall)*
    Anadin Preps [NB. Contains
    caffeine] *(Whitehall)*
    Angettes *(Bristol-Myers)*
PoM Apsifen *(APS)*
    Askit Powders, Tablets [NB.
    Contains caffeine] *(Askit)*
PoM Aspirin *(Unbranded)*
    Aspro Preps *(Nicholas)*
    Banimax *(SmithKline Beecham)*
    Beechams Powders, Powders
    Tablets (NOT Powders
    Capsules) [NB. Contains
    caffeine] *(Beecham)*
    Benoral *(Sterling Winthrop)*
PoM Brufen *(Boots)*
    Cafadol [NB. Contains caffeine]
    (Typharm)

Calpol *(Wellcome)*
Caprin *(Sinclair)*
Contrapain *(Nicholas)*
Cullens Headache Powders [NB. Contains caffeine] *(Cullen & Davidson)*
Cupanol *(Cupal)*
Cuprofen *(Cupal)*
De Witt's Analgesic Pills [NB. Contains caffeine] *(De Witt)*
Disprin Preps *(Reckitt & Colman)*
Disprol *(Reckitt & Colman)*
Doan's Extra Strength Backache Pills *(Ciba)*
PoM Dolobid *(Morson)*
PoM Dysman *(Ashbourne)*
Fanalgic *(Mitchell)*
Femafen *(Nicholas)*
PoM Fenbid Spansule *(SK&F)*
Fenning's Adult Powders [NB. Contains caffeine] *(Fennings)*
Fenning's Children's Cooling Powders *(Fennings)*
PoM Fenopron *(Dista)*
Fynnon Calcium Aspirin *(SmithKline Beecham)*
Hedex *(Sterling Health)*
PoM Ibufac *(DDSA)*
Inoven *(Janssen)*
PoM Ibuprofen *(Unbranded)*
PoM Junifen *(Boots)*
Junior Panaleve *(Leo)*
PoM Laboprin *(LAB)*
Librofem *(Ciba)*
PoM Medised *(Panpharma)*
Migraclear *(Nicholas)*
Migrafen *(Chatfield)*
PoM Motrin *(Upjohn)*
Novaprin *(Pharmexco)*
Nu-Seals Aspirin *(Lilly)*
Nurofen *(Crookes)*
Nurse Sykes Powder [NB. Contains caffeine] *(Waterhouse)*
Pacifene *(Sussex)*
Paldesic *(RP Drugs)*
Pameton *(Sterling Winthrop)*
Panadol Tablets, Capsules, Soluble, Junior, Baby & Infant *(Sterling Winthrop)*
Panadol Extra [NB. Contains caffeine] *(Sterling Health)*
Panaleve *(Leo)*
Paracetamol Tablets *(Unbranded)*
Paracets *(Sussex)*
Paraclear *(Nicholas)*
Paramin *(Wallis)*
Phensic [NB. Contains caffeine] *(Beecham)*
Platet Cleartab *(Nicholas)*
PoM Ponstan *(Parke Davis)*
Powerin [NB. Contains caffeine] *(Whitehall)*

Proflex, Proflex SR *(Ciba)*
PoM Progesic *(Lilly)*
Relcofen *(Cox)*
Resolve *(SmithKline Beecham)*
PoM Rimafen *(Rima)*
Salzone *(Wallace)*
Seclodin *(Whitehall)*
Solprin *(Reckitt & Colman)*
PoM Synflex *(Syntex)*
PoM Tegretol *(Geigy)*
Toptabs [NB. Contains caffeine] *(Sussex)*
Tramil *(Whitehall)*

(b) Hypnotics

Some international federations, eg. modern pentathlon, do not allow the use of sedatives. Check, well before the event

PoM Amytal [CD] *(Lilly)*
PoM Dalmane *(Roche)*
PoM Dormonoct *(Roussel)*
PoM Halcion *(Upjohn)*
PoM Heminevrin *(Astra)*
PoM Hespan *(Du Pont)*
PoM Loprazolam *(Unbranded)*
PoM Lormetazepam *(Unbranded)*
PoM Mogadon *(Roche)*
PoM Nitrados *(Berk)*
PoM Nitrazepam *(Unbranded)*
PoM Noctec *(Squibb)*
PoM Normison *(Wyeth)*
PoM Paxane *(Mercury)*
PoM Remnos *(DDSA)*
PoM Rohypnol *(Roche)*
PoM Seconal Sodium [CD] *(Lilly)* ·
PoM Sodium Amytal [CD] *(Lilly)*
Sominex *(Beecham Health Care)*
PoM Somnite *(Norgine)*
PoM Soneryl [CD] *(May & Baker)*
PoM Surem *(Galen)*
PoM Temazepam *(Unbranded)*
PoM Trancopal *(Sterling Winthrop)*
PoM Triazolam *(Unbranded)*
PoM Tuinal [CD] *(Lilly)*
PoM Unisomnia *(Unigreg)*
PoM Welldorm *(SNP)*
PoM Zimovane *(Rhone-Poulenc)*

(c) Anxiolytics

PoM Almazine *(Steinhard)*
PoM Alupram *(Steinhard)*
PoM Atarax *(Pfizer)*
PoM Atensine *(Berk)*
PoM Ativan *(Wyeth)*
PoM Buspar *(Bristol-Myers)*
PoM Chlordiazepoxide *(Unbranded)*
PoM Diazemuls *(Dumex)*
PoM Diazepam *(Unbranded)*
PoM Equanil [CD] *(Wyeth)*
PoM Frisium *(Hoechst/Albert)*
PoM Integrin *(Sterling Winthrop)*

PoM Lexotan *(Roche)*
PoM Librium *(Roche)*
PoM Lorazepam *(Unbranded)*
PoM Motipress *(Squibb)*
PoM Motival *(Squibb)*
PoM Nobrium *(Roche)*
PoM Oxanid *(Steinhard)*
PoM Oxazepam *(Unbranded)*
PoM Solis *(Galen)*
PoM Stelazine *(SK&F)*
PoM Stesolid *(CP Pharm)*
PoM Tensium *(DDSA)*
PoM Tranxene *(Boehringer Ing.)*
PoM Tropium *(DDSA)*
PoM Valium *(Roche)*
PoM Xanax *(Upjohn)*

(d) Antipsychotics

PoM Anquil *(Janssen)*
PoM Clopixol *(Lundbeck)*
PoM Clozaril *(Sandoz)*
PoM Depixol *(Lundbeck)*
PoM Dolmatil *(Squibb)*
PoM Dozic *(RP Drugs)*
PoM Droleptan *(Janssen)*
PoM Fentazin *(Allen & Hanburys)*
PoM Fortunan *(Steinhard)*
PoM Haldol Decanoate *(Janssen)*
PoM Heminevrin *(Astra)*
PoM Integrin *(Sterling Winthrop)*
PoM Largactil *(May & Baker)*
PoM Loxapac *(Lederle)*
PoM Melleril *(Sandoz)*
PoM Modecate *(Squibb)*
PoM Moditen *(Squibb)*
PoM Neulactil *(May & Baker)*
PoM Nozinan *(May & Baker)*
PoM Orap *(Janssen)*
PoM Piportil Depot *(May & Baker)*
PoM Redeptin *(SK&F)*
PoM Serenace *(Searle)*
PoM Sparine *(Wyeth)*
PoM Stelazine *(SK&F)*
PoM Stemetil *(May & Baker)*
PoM Sulpitil *(Tillotts)*
PoM Triperidol *(Lagap)*
PoM Triptafen *(Allen & Hanburys)*

(e) Antidepressants

PoM Allegron *(Dista)*
PoM Amitriptyline *(Unbranded)*
PoM Anafranil *(Geigy)*
PoM Asendis *(Lederle)*
PoM Aventyl *(Lilly)*
PoM Bolvidon *(Organon)*
PoM Camcolit *(Norgine)*
PoM Concordin *(MSD)*
PoM Domical *(Berk)*
PoM Evadyne *(Wyeth)*
PoM Faverin *(Duphar)*
PoM Fluanxol *(Lundbeck)*
PoM Gamanil *(Merck)*
PoM Imipramine *(Unbranded)*

PoM Lentizol *(Parke Davis)*
PoM Limbitrol 5 *(Roche)*
PoM Liskonum *(SK&F)*
PoM Litarex *(CP Pharm)*
PoM Ludiomil *(Ciba)*
PoM Lustral *(Invicta)*
PoM Marplan *(Roche)*
PoM Molipaxin *(Roussel)*
PoM Motipress *(Squibb)*
PoM Motival *(Squibb)*
PoM Nardil *(Parke Davis)*
PoM Norval *(Bencard)*
PoM Parnate *(SK&F)*
PoM Parstelin *(SK&F)*
PoM Pertofran *(Geigy)*
PoM Phasal *(Lagap)*
PoM Priadel *(Delandale)*
PoM Prondol *(Wyeth)*
PoM Prothiaden *(Boots)*
PoM Prozac *(Dista)*
PoM Seroxat *(SmithKline Beecham)*
PoM Sinequan *(Pfizer)*
PoM Surmontil *(May & Baker)*
PoM Tegretol *(Geigy)*
PoM Tofranil *(Geigy)*
PoM Triptafen *(Allen & Hanburys)*
PoM Tryptizol *(Morson)*
PoM Vivalan *(ICI)*

(f) CNS Stimulants

All CNS stimulants are banned

(g) Movement disorders

PoM Akineton *(Knoll)*
PoM Arpicolin *(RP Drugs)*
PoM Artane *(Lederle)*
PoM Bentex *(Steinhard)*
PoM Biorphen *(Bioglan)*
PoM Brocadopa *(Brocades)*
PoM Broflex *(Bioglan)*
PoM Cogentin *(MSD)*
PoM Disipal *(Brocades)*
PoM Eldepryl *(Britannia)*
PoM Kemadrin *(Wellcome)*
PoM Larodopa *(Roche)*
PoM Madopar *(Roche)*
PoM Mantadine *(Du Pont)*
PoM Nitoman *(Roche)*
PoM Parlodel *(Sandoz)*
PoM Procyclidine *(Unbranded)*
PoM Revanil *(Roche)*
PoM Sinemet *(Du Pont)*
PoM Symmetrel *(Geigy)*
PoM Tremonil *(Sandoz)*

(h) Anticonvulsants

PoM Ativan Injection *(Wyeth)*
PoM Clobazam *(Unbranded)*
PoM Diazemuls *(Dumex)*
PoM Emeside *(LAB)*
PoM Epanutin *(Parke Davis)*
PoM Epilim *(Sanofi)*
PoM Frisium *(Hoechst/Albert)*

PoM Gardenal Sodium [CD] *(May & Baker)*
PoM Heminevrin IV Infusion *(Astra)*
PoM Mysoline *(ICI)*
PoM Prominal [CD] *(Sterling Winthrop)*
PoM Rivotril *(Roche)*
PoM Sabril *(Merrell Dow)*
PoM Sodium Amytal [CD] *(Lilly)*
PoM Stesolid *(CP Pharm)*
PoM Tegretol *(Geigy)*
PoM Valium Injection *(Roche)*
PoM Zarontin *(Parke Davis)*

(i) Anti-emetics

Avomine *(May & Baker)*
PoM Buccastem *(Reckitt & Colman)*
PoM Cesamet *(Lilly)*
Dramamine *(Searle)*
PoM Gastrobid Continus *(Napp)*
PoM Gastroflux *(Ashbourne)*
PoM Gastromax *(Farmitalia)*
Joy-rides *(Stafford Miller)*
Kwells *(Nicholas)*
Marzine RF *(Wellcome)*
PoM Maxolon *(Beecham)*
PoM Metox *(Steinhard)*
PoM Metramid *(Nicholas)*
PoM Motilium *(Sterling Winthrop)*
PoM Mygdalon *(DDSA)*
PoM Parmid *(Lagap)*
PoM Primperan *(Berk)*
PoM Scopoderm *(Ciba)*
Sea-legs *(Crookes)*
PoM Serc *(Duphar)*
PoM Stelazine *(SK&F)*
PoM Stemetil *(May & Baker)*
Stugeron *(Janssen)*
PoM Torecan *(Sandoz)*
PoM Valoid *(Wellcome)*
PoM Vertigon Spansule *(SK&F)*
PoM Zofran *(Glaxo)*

5. Musculoskeletal System

(a) Nonsteroidal anti-inflammatory, antirheumatoid agents

PoM Alrheumat *(Bayer)*
PoM Apsifen *(APS)*
PoM Arthrofen *(Ashbourne)*
PoM Arthrosin *(Ashbourne)*
PoM Artracin *(DDSA)*
Benoral *(Sterling Winthrop)*
PoM Brufen *(Boots)*
PoM Butacote *(Geigy)*
Caprin *(Sinclair)*
PoM Clinoril *(MSD)*
PoM Disalcid *(3M Health Care)*
PoM Distamine *(Dista)*
PoM Dolobid *(Morson)*
PoM Dysman *(Ashbourne)*

PoM Ebufac *(Ashbourne)*
PoM Emflex *(Merck)*
PoM Feldene *(Pfizer)*
PoM Fenbid Spansule *(SK&F)*
PoM Fenopron *(Dista)*
PoM Flexin Continus *(Napp)*
PoM Froben *(Boots)*
PoM Ibuprofen *(Unbranded)*
PoM Ibular *(Lagap)*
PoM Imbrilon *(Berk)*
PoM Indocid *(Morson)*
PoM Indolar SR *(Lagap)*
PoM Indomax *(Ashbourne)*
PoM Indomethacin *(Unbranded)*
PoM Indomod *(Pharmacia)*
PoM Laraflex *(Lagap)*
PoM Larapam *(Lagap)*
PoM Lederfen *(Lederle)*
PoM Lidifen *(Berk)*
PoM Lodine *(Wyeth)*
PoM Mobiflex *(Roche)*
PoM Mobilan *(Galen)*
PoM Motrin *(Upjohn)*
PoM Myocrisin *(Rorer)*
PoM Naprosyn *(Syntex)*
PoM Naproxen *(Unbranded)*
Nivaquine *(May & Baker)*
Nu-Seals Aspirin *(Lilly)*
PoM Nycopren *(Lundbeck)*
PoM Orudis *(May & Baker)*
PoM Oruvail *(May & Baker)*
PoM Palaprin Forte *(Nicholas)*
PoM Paxofen *(Mercury)*
PoM Pendramine *(Degussa)*
PoM Piroxicam *(Unbranded)*
PoM Plaquenil *(Sterling Winthrop)*
Ponstan, Ponstan Forte *(Parke Davis)*
PoM Progesic *(Lilly)*
PoM Relifex *(Bencard)*
PoM Rheumox *(Wyeth)*
PoM Rhumalgan *(Lagap)*
PoM Ridaura *(Bridge)*
PoM Salazopyrin EN-Tabs *(Pharmacia)*
PoM Slo-Indo *(Generics)*
Solprin *(Reckitt & Colman)*
PoM Surgam SA *(Roussel)*
PoM Synflex *(Syntex)*
PoM Tolectin *(Cilag)*
PoM Trilisate *(Napp)*
PoM Valenac *(Shire)*
PoM Volraman *(Eastern)*
PoM Voltarol *(Ciba-Geigy)*

(b) Muscle relaxants

PoM Alupram *(Steinhard)*
PoM Atensine *(Berk)*
PoM Carisoma *(Pharmax)*
PoM Dantrium *(Norwich Eaton)*
PoM Diazemuls *(Dumex)*
PoM Lioresal *(Ciba)*
PoM Lobak *(Sterling Winthrop)*
PoM Norflex *(3M Health Care)*

PoM = Prescription-only Medicines

PoM Robaxin *(Wyeth)*
PoM Robaxisal Forte *(Wyeth)*
PoM Stesolid *(CP Pharm)*
PoM Tensium *(DDSA)*
PoM Valium *(Roche)*

(c) Rubefacients, topical analgesics/NSAIDs

Algesal *(Duphar)*
Algipan *(Wyeth)*
Aradolene *(Fisons CH)*
Aspellin *(Fisons CH)*
Balmosa *(Pharmax)*
Bayolin *(Bayer)*
Bengue's Balsam *(Chancellor)*
Cremalgin *(Rorer)*
Difflam *(3M Health Care)*
Dubam *(Norma)*
PoM Feldene Gel *(Pfizer)*
Finalgon *(Boehringer Ing.)*
Ibuleve *(Dendron)*
Intralgin *(3M Health Care)*
PoM Movelat *(Panpharma)*
Proflex *(Zyma)*
Ralgex *(SmithKline Beecham)*
Salonair *(Salonpas)*
Transvasin *(Lloyds)*
PoM Traxam *(Lederle)*
PoM Voltarol Emulgel *(Geigy)*

(d) Agents used in gout and hyperuricaemia

PoM Allopurinol *(Unbranded)*
PoM Aloral *(Lagap)*
PoM Aluline *(Steinhard)*
PoM Anturan *(Geigy)*
PoM Caplenal *(Berk)*
PoM Cosuric *(DDSA)*
PoM Hamarin *(Nicholas)*
PoM Rheumox *(Wyeth)*
PoM Zyloric *(Wellcome)*

6. Hormones

(a) Sex hormones, anabolic agents

PoM Androcur *(Schering HC)*
PoM Cyclo-Progynova *(Schering HC)*
PoM Cyclogest *(Hoechst)*
PoM Depo-Provera 50 mg/mL *(Upjohn)*
PoM Depostat *(Schering HC)*
PoM Dimetriose *(Roussel)*
PoM Duphaston *(Duphar)*
PoM Estraderm *(Ciba)*
PoM Estrapak *(Ciba)*
PoM Gestanin *(Organon)*
PoM Gestone *(Paines & Byrne)*
PoM Harmogen *(Abbott)*
PoM Hormonin *(Shire)*
PoM Menophase *(Syntex)*

PoM Menzol *(Kabi)*
PoM Modrenal *(Wanskerne)*
PoM Ortho Dienoestrol *(Cilag)*
PoM Ortho-Gynest *(Cilag)*
PoM Ovestin *(Organon)*
PoM Premarin *(Wyeth)*
PoM Prempak-C *(Wyeth)*
PoM Primolut N *(Schering HC)*
PoM Progynova *(Schering HC)*
PoM Proluton Depot *(Schering HC)*
PoM Provera *(Upjohn)*
PoM Tampovagan Stilboestrol and Lactic Acid *(Norgine)*
PoM Trisequens *(Novo Nordisk)*
PoM Utovlan *(Syntex)*
PoM Vagifem *(Novo)*

(b) Corticosteroid hormones

Corticosteroid hormones that are used topically, or by inhalation are permitted

Local or intra-articular injections may be administered but require written permission

PoM Adcortyl *(Princeton)*
PoM Decadron Inj *(MSD)*
PoM Deltastab Inj *(Boots)*
PoM Depo-Medrone with Lidocaine *(Upjohn)*
PoM Hydrocortistab Inj. *(Boots)*
PoM Lederspan 20 mg *(Lederle)*

(c) Trophic hormones

PoM Clomid *(Merrell Dow)*
PoM DDAVP *(Ferring)*
PoM Desmospray *(Ferring)*
PoM Glypressin *(Ferring)*
PoM Humegon *(Organon)*
PoM Metrodin *(Serono)*
PoM Noltam *(Lederle)*
PoM Nolvadex-D *(ICI)*
PoM Parlodel *(Sandoz)*
PoM Pergonal *(Serono)*
PoM Pitressin *(Parke Davis)*
PoM Rehibin *(Serono)*
PoM Serophene *(Serono)*
PoM Syntopressin *(Sandoz)*
PoM Tamofen *(Tillotts)*
PoM Tamoxifen *(Unbranded)*
PoM TRH *(Roche)*

(d) Insulin, hypoglycaemic agents

PoM Calabren *(Berk)*
PoM Daonil *(Hoechst)*
PoM Diabinese *(Pfizer)*
PoM Diamicron *(Servier)*
PoM Eudemine *(Allen & Hanburys)*
PoM Euglucon *(Roussel)*
PoM Glibenclamide *(Unbranded)*
PoM Glibenese *(Pfizer)*
PoM Glucagon *(Lilly)*

PoM Glucagon *(Novo)*
PoM Glucophage *(Lipha)*
PoM Glurenorm *(Sterling Winthrop)*
Guarem *(Rybar)*
Guarina *(Norgine)*
Human Actraphane *(Novo Nordisk)*
Human Actrapid *(Novo Nordisk)*
Human Initard 50/50 *(Nordisk & Wellcome)*
Human Insulatard *(Nordisk & Wellcome)*
Human Mixtard 30/70 *(Nordisk & Wellcome)*
Human Monotard *(Novo Nordisk)*
Human Protaphane *(Novo Nordisk)*
Human Ultratard *(Novo Nordisk)*
Human Velosulin *(Nordisk & Wellcome)*
Humulin I *(Lilly)*
Humulin Lente *(Lilly)*
Humulin M1 *(Lilly)*
Humulin M2 *(Lilly)*
Humulin M3 *(Lilly)*
Humulin M4 *(Lilly)*
Humulin S *(Lilly)*
Humulin Zn *(Lilly)*
Hypurin Isophane *(CP Pharm)*
Hypurin Lente *(CP Pharm)*
Hypurin Neutral *(CP Pharm)*
Hypurin Protamine Zinc *(CP Pharm)*
Initard 50/50 *(Nordisk & Wellcome)*
Insulatard *(Nordisk & Wellcome)*
Lentard MC *(Novo Nordisk)*
PoM Libanil *(APS)*
PoM Malix *(Lagap)*
PoM Metformin *(Unbranded)*
PoM Minodiab *(Farmitalia)*
Mixtard 30/70 *(Nordisk & Wellcome)*
PoM Orabet *(Lagap)*
Penmix 30/70 *(Novo Nordisk)*
Rapitard MC *(Novo Nordisk)*
PoM Rastinon *(Hoechst)*
PoM Semi-Daonil *(Hoechst)*
Semitard MC *(Novo Nordisk)*
PoM Tolanase *(Upjohn)*
Velosulin *(Nordisk & Wellcome)*

(e) Thyroid and antithyroid agents

PoM Eltroxin *(Glaxo)*
PoM Neo-Mercazole *(Nicholas)*
PoM Tertroxin *(Glaxo)*
PoM Thyroxine *(Unbranded)*

(f) Other hormonal agents

PoM Aredia *(Ciba)*
PoM Calcitare *(Rorer)*

PoM Calsynar *(Rorer)*
PoM Didronel *(Norwich Eaton)*
PoM Loron *(BM Pharm)*
PoM Miacalcic *(Sandoz)*

7. Genitourinary System

(a) Oral and topical vaginal antiinfective medication

Aci-Jel *(Cilag)*
Betadine *(Napp)*
PoM Canesten *(Baypharm)*
PoM Condyline *Brocades*
PoM Diflucan *(Pfizer)*
PoM Ecostatin *(Princeton)*
PoM Flagyl *(May & Baker)*
PoM Gynatren *(Solco Basle)*
PoM Gyno-Daktarin *(Janssen)*
PoM Gyno-Pevaryl *(Cilag)*
PoM Imunovir *(Leo)*
PoM Intron A *(Schering-Plough)*
PoM Metrolyl *(Lagap)*
PoM Monistat *(Cilag)*
Naxogin 500 *(Farmitalia)*
PoM Nizoral *(Janssen)*
PoM Nystan *(Princeton)*
Pevaryl *(Cilag)*
PoM Pimafucin *(Brocades)*
PoM Sporanox *(Janssen)*
PoM Sultrin *(Cilag)*
PoM Travogyn *(Schering HC)*
PoM Warticon *(Kabi)*
PoM Zadstat *(Lederle)*
PoM Zovirax *(Wellcome)*

(b) Urinary tract infections including urinary antiseptics, alkalinisers

PoM Cinobac *(Lilly)*
Effercitrate *(Typharm)*
PoM Furadantin *(Norwich Eaton)*
Hiprex *(3M Health Care)*
PoM Macrodantin *(Norwich Eaton)*
PoM Mictral *(Sterling Winthrop)*
PoM Negram *(Sterling Winthrop)*
PoM Uriben *(RP Drugs)*
Urisal *(Sterling Winthrop)*
PoM Utinor *(MSD)*

(c) Renal and bladder disorders

Calcisorb *(3M Health Care)*
PoM Desmospray *(Ferring)*
PoM Ditropan *(Smith & Nephew)*
PoM Doralese *(Bridge)*
PoM Hypovase *(Invicta)*
PoM Instillagel *(CliniMed)*
PoM Micturin *(Kabi)*
PoM Myotonine *(Glenwood)*
PoM Noxyflex S *(Geistlich)*

PoM Polybactrin Soluble GU *(Wellcome)*
PoM Pro-Banthine *(Gold Cross)*
PoM Prostigmin *(Roche)*
PoM Rimso-50 *(Britannia)*
PoM Rowatinex *(Monmouth)*
PoM Ubretid *(Rorer)*
Uriflex *(Galen)*
PoM Urispas *(Syntex)*
Uro-Tainer Preps *(CliniMed)*
PoM Uromitexan *(Degussa)*
Xylocaine Gel *(Astra)*

(d) Dysmenorrhoea, menorrhagia and uterine relaxants

PoM Buscopan *(Boehringer Ing.)*
PoM Cervagem *(May & Baker)*
PoM Cyklokapron *(Kabi)*
PoM Dicynene *(Delandale)*
PoM Duvadilan *(Duphar)*
PoM Dysman *(Ashbourne)*
PoM Efamast *(Scotia)*
PoM Epifoam *(Stafford-Miller)*
PoM Hemabate *(Upjohn)*
PoM Ponstan, Ponstan Forte *(Parke Davis)*
PoM Prepidil *(Upjohn)*
PoM Propess *(Roussel)*
PoM Prostin E$_2$ *(Upjohn)*
PoM Prostin F$_2$ Alpha *(Upjohn)*
Spasmonal *(Norgine)*
PoM Syntocinon *(Sandoz)*
PoM Syntometrine *(Sandoz)*

8. Infections and Infestations

(a) Antibiotics and antibacterials

PoM Achromycin *(Lederle)*
PoM Aerosporin *(Wellcome)*
PoM Almodan *(Berk)*
PoM Ambaxin *(Upjohn)*
PoM Amfipen *(Brocades)*
PoM Amikin *(Bristol-Myers)*
PoM Amoram *(Eastern)*
PoM Amoxil *(Bencard)*
PoM Amoxycillin *(Unbranded)*
PoM Ampicillin *(Unbranded)*
PoM Ampiclox *(Beecham)*
PoM Apsin VK *(APS)*
PoM Arpimycin *(RP Drugs)*
PoM Augmentin *(Beecham)*
PoM Aureomycin *(Lederle)*
PoM Azactam *(Squibb)*
PoM Bactrim *(Roche)*
PoM Baxan *(Bristol-Myers)*
PoM Baypen *(Bayer)*
PoM Berkmycen *(Berk)*
PoM Bicillin *(Brocades)*
PoM Cefizox *(Wellcome)*

PoM Celbenin *(Beecham)*
PoM Ceporex *(Glaxo)*
PoM Chemotrim Paed. *(RP Drugs)*
PoM Chloromycetin *(Parke Davis)*
PoM Cidomycin *(Roussel)*
PoM Ciproxin *(Baypharm)*
PoM Claforan *(Roussel)*
PoM Co-Trimoxazole *(Unbranded)*
PoM Colomycin *(Pharmax)*
PoM Comox *(Norton)*
PoM Comprecin *(Parke Davis)*
PoM Crystapen *(Glaxo)*
PoM Dalacin C *(Upjohn)*
PoM Deteclo *(Lederle)*
PoM Dicapen *(Leo)*
PoM Distaclor *(Dista)*
PoM Distaquaine V-K *(Dista)*
PoM Elyzol *(CP Pharm)*
PoM Enteromide *(Consolidated)*
PoM Eradacin *(Sterling Winthrop)*
PoM Erycen *(Berk)*
PoM Erymax *(Parke Davis)*
PoM Erythrocin *(Abbott)*
PoM Erythromid *(Abbott)*
PoM Erythromycin *(Unbranded)*
PoM Erythroped *(Abbott)*
PoM Fasigyn *(Pfizer)*
PoM Fectrim, Fectrim Forte *(DDSA)*
PoM Flagyl *(May & Baker)*
PoM Floxapen *(Beecham)*
PoM Flu-Amp *(Generics)*
PoM Fluclomix *(Ashbourne)*
PoM Flucloxacillin *(Unbranded)*
PoM Fortum *(Glaxo)*
PoM Fucidin *(Leo)*
PoM Galenamox *(Galen)*
PoM Garamycin Paed. *(Schering-Plough)*
PoM Genticin *(Nicholas)*
PoM Ilosone *(Dista)*
PoM Imperacin *(ICI)*
PoM Ipral *(Squibb)*
PoM Kannasyn *(Sterling Winthrop)*
PoM Kefadol *(Dista)*
PoM Keflex *(Lilly)*
PoM Keflin *(Lilly)*
PoM Kefzol *(Lilly)*
PoM Kelfizine W *(Farmitalia)*
PoM Kemicetine Succinate *(Farmitalia)*
PoM Ladropen *(Berk)*
PoM Laratrim *(Lagap)*
PoM Ledermycin *(Lederle)*
PoM Lincocin *(Upjohn)*
PoM Magnapen *(Beecham)*
PoM Mefoxin *(MSD)*
PoM Megaclor *(Pharmax)*
PoM Metrolyl *(Lagap)*
PoM Metronidazole *(Unbranded)*
PoM Minocin *(Lederle)*
PoM Miraxid *(Fisons)*
PoM Monaspor *(Ciba)*
PoM Monotrim *(Duphar)*
PoM Moxalactam *(Lilly)*
PoM Mycifradin *(Upjohn)*

PoM = Prescription-only Medicines

PoM Mysteclin *(Squibb)*
PoM Nebcin *(Lilly)*
PoM Negram *(Sterling Winthrop)*
PoM Netillin *(Schering-Plough)*
PoM Nidazol *(Steinhard)*
PoM Nivemycin *(Boots)*
PoM Nordox *(Panpharma)*
PoM Orbenin *(Beecham)*
PoM Oxytetracycline *(Unbranded)*
PoM Panmycin *(Upjohn)*
PoM Penbritin *(Beecham)*
PoM Penicillin VK *(Unbranded)*
PoM Penidural *(Wyeth)*
PoM Pentacarinat *(Rorer)*
PoM Pentostam *(Wellcome)*
PoM Pipril *(Lederle)*
PoM Pondocillin *(Leo)*
PoM Primaxin *(MSD)*
PoM Pyopen *(Beecham)*
PoM Reticin *(DDSA)*
PoM Rifadin *(Merrell Dow)*
PoM Rimactane *(Ciba)*
PoM Securopen *(Bayer)*
PoM Selexid *(Leo)*
PoM Selexidin *(Leo)*
PoM Septrin *(Wellcome)*
PoM Soframycin *(Roussel)*
PoM Stabillin V-K *(Boots)*
PoM Stafoxil *(Brocades)*
PoM Suprax *(Lederle)*
PoM Sustamycin *(BM Pharm)*
PoM Syraprim *(Wellcome)*
PoM Talpen *(Beecham)*
PoM Targocid *(Merrell Dow)*
PoM Tarivid *(Hoechst)*
PoM Temopen *(Bencard)*
PoM Terramycin *(Pfizer)*
PoM Tetrabid *(Organon)*
PoM Tetrachel *(Berk)*
PoM Tetracycline *(Unbranded)*
PoM Tetralysal *(Farmitalia)*
PoM Tetrex *(Bristol-Myers)*
PoM Ticar *(Beecham)*
PoM Tiempe *(DDSA)*
PoM Timentin *(Beecham)*
PoM Trimethoprim *(Unbranded)*
PoM Trimogal *(Lagap)*
PoM Trimopan *(Berk)*
PoM Triplopen *(Glaxo)*
PoM Trobicin *(Upjohn)*
PoM Uriben *(RP Drugs)*
PoM V-CIL-K *(Lilly)*
PoM Vancocin CP, Matrigel *(Lilly)*
PoM Velosef *(Squibb)*
PoM Vibramycin *(Invicta)*
PoM Vidopen *(Berk)*
PoM Zadstat *(Lederle)*
PoM Zinacef *(Glaxo)*
PoM Zinnat *(Glaxo)*

(b) Antifungals

PoM Alcobon *(Roche)*
PoM Daktarin *(Janssen)*
PoM Diflucan *(Pfizer)*

PoM Entamizole *(Boots)*
PoM Fulcin *(ICI)*
PoM Fungilin *(Squibb)*
PoM Fungizone *(Squibb)*
PoM Furamide *(Boots)*
PoM Grisovin *(Glaxo)*
PoM Nizoral *(Janssen)*
PoM Nystan *(Princeton)*
PoM Sporanox *(Janssen)*

(c) Antituberculous, antileprotics

PoM Capastat *(Dista)*
PoM Dapsone *(Unbranded)*
PoM Lamprene *(Geigy)*
PoM Myambutol *(Lederle)*
PoM Mynah *(Lederle)*
PoM Rifadin *(Merrell Dow)*
PoM Rifater *(Merrell Dow)*
PoM Rifinah *(Merrell Dow)*
PoM Rimactane *(Ciba)*
PoM Rimactazid *(Ciba)*
PoM Rimifon *(Roche)*
PoM Zinamide *(MSD)*

(d) Antimalarials

PoM Avloclor *(ICI)*
Daraprim *(Wellcome)*
PoM Fansidar *(Roche)*
PoM Lariam *(Roche)*
PoM Maloprim *(Wellcome)*
Nivaquine *(May & Baker)*
Paludrine *(ICI)*

(e) Antivirals

PoM Cymevene *(Syntex)*
PoM Foscavir *(Astra)*
PoM Herpid *(Boehringer Ing.)*
PoM Iduridin *(Nordic)*
PoM Imunovir *(Leo)*
PoM Retrovir *(Wellcome)*
PoM Symmetrel *(Geigy)*
PoM Vira-A *(Parke Davis)*
PoM Virazid *(Britannia)*
PoM Virudox *(Bioglan)*
PoM Zovirax *(Wellcome)*

(f) Anthelmintics and amoebicides

Alcopar *(Wellcome)*
Antepar *(Wellcome)*
PoM Avloclor *(ICI)*
Banocide *(Wellcome)*
PoM Combantrin *(Pfizer)*
PoM Flagyl *(May & Baker)*
PoM Metrolyl *(Lagap)*
PoM Mintezol *(MSD)*
Pripsen *(Reckitt & Colman)*
PoM Vansil *(Pfizer)*
PoM Vermox *(Janssen)*
Yomesan *(Bayer)*
PoM Zadstat *(Lederle)*

9. Neoplastic Disorders

PoM Aclacin *(Lundbeck)*
PoM Alexan *(Pfizer)*
PoM Alkeran *(Wellcome)*
PoM Amsidine *(Parke Davis)*
PoM BicNu *(Bristol-Myers)*
PoM CCNU *(Lundbeck)*
PoM Coparvax *(Wellcome)*
PoM Cosmegen Lyovac *(MSD)*
PoM Cyprostat *(Schering HC)*
PoM Cytosar *(Upjohn)*
PoM Depo-Provera 150 mg/mL
(Upjohn)
PoM Depostat *(Schering HC)*
PoM Drogenil *(Schering-Plough)*
PoM DTIC-Dome *(Bayer)*
PoM Efudix *(Roche)*
PoM Eldisine *(Lilly)*
PoM Emblon *(Berk)*
PoM Endoxana *(Degussa)*
PoM Estracyt *(Pharmacia)*
PoM Estradurin *(Pharmacia)*
PoM Farlutal *(Farmitalia)*
PoM Honvan *(Boehringer Ing.)*
PoM Hydrea *(Squibb)*
PoM Intron A *(Schering-Plough)*
PoM Lanvis *(Wellcome)*
PoM Leukeran *(Wellcome)*
PoM Maxtrex *(Farmitalia)*
PoM Megace *(Bristol-Myers)*
PoM Mithracin *(Pfizer)*
PoM Mitoxana *(Degussa)*
PoM Myelobromol *(Sinclair)*
PoM Myleran *(Wellcome)*
PoM Natulan *(Roche)*
PoM Noltam *(Lederle)*
PoM Nolvadex-D *(ICI)*
PoM Novantrone *(Lederle)*
PoM Oncovin *(Lilly)*
PoM Orimeten *(Ciba)*
PoM Paraplatin *(Bristol-Myers)*
PoM Pharmorubicin *(Farmitalia)*
PoM Provera *(Upjohn)*
PoM Puri-Nethol *(Wellcome)*
PoM Razoxin *(ICI)*
PoM Roferon-A *(Roche)*
PoM Sandostatin *(Sandoz)*
PoM SH 420 *(Schering HC)*
PoM Tamofen *(Tillotts)*
PoM Tamoxifen *(Unbranded)*
PoM Velbe *(Lilly)*
PoM Vepesid *(Bristol-Myers)*
PoM Wellferon *(Wellcome)*
PoM Zavedos *(Farmitalia)*

10. Nutrition and Metabolism

(a) Infant formulas, supplemental and enteral nutrition

Aglutella *(Nutricia)*
AI 110 *(Nestle)*
Albumaid *(SHS)*
Alembicol D *(Alembic)*
Alfare *(Nestle)*
Aminex *(Cow & Gate)*
Aminogran *(UCB)*
Analog *(SHS)*
Aproten *(Ultrapharm)*
Bi-Aglut *(Ultrapharm)*
Calogen *(SHS)*
Caloreen *(Roussel)*
Carobel Instant *(Cow & Gate)*
Casilan *(Farley)*
Clinifeed *(Roussel)*
Dialamine *(SHS)*
Duocal *(SHS)*
Elemental 028 *(SHS)*
Ener-G *(General Designs)*
Enrich *(Abbott)*
Ensure *(Abbott)*
Flexical *(Mead Johnson)*
Forceval Protein *(Unigreg)*
Formula MCT (1) *(Cow & Gate)*
Formula S *(Cow & Gate)*
Fortical *(Cow & Gate)*
Fortisip *(Cow & Gate)*
Fortison *(Cow & Gate)*
Fresubin *(Fresenius)*
Galactomin 17 & 19 *(Cow & Gate)*
Generaid *(SHS)*
Glutafin *(Nutricia)*
Glutenex *(Cow & Gate)*
Hepatic Aid II *(Kendall)*
Hycal *(Beecham Products)*
Isocal *(Mead Johnson)*
Isomil *(Abbott)*
Juvela *(Nutricia)*
Liga *(Cow & Gate)*
Liquigen *(SHS)*
Liquisorb *(Merck)*
Liquisorbon MCT *(Merck)*
Locasol *(Cow & Gate)*
Lofenalac *(Mead Johnson)*
MSUD Aid *(SHS)*
Maxamaid *(SHS)*
Maxamum XP *(SHS)*
Maxijul *(SHS)*
Maxipro HBV Super Soluble *(SHS)*
MCT Pepdite *(SHS)*
Metabolic Mineral Mixture *(SHS)*
Milupa lpd *(Milupa)*
Minafen *(Cow & Gate)*
Neocate *(SHS)*

Nestargel *(Nestle)*
Nutramigen *(Mead Johnson)*
Osmolite *(Abbott)*
Ostersoy *(Farley)*
Paediasure *(Abbott)*
Pepdite *(SHS)*
Peptamen *(Clintec)*
Pepti-2000 LF *(Cow & Gate)*
Pepti-Junior *(Cow & Gate)*
Peptisorb *(Merck)*
Peptisorbon *(Merck)*
PK Aid III *(SHS)*
PKU 2, PKU 3 *(Milupa)*
PKU Drink *(Nutricia)*
Polial *(Ultrapharm)*
Polycal *(Cow & Gate)*
Polycose *(Abbott)*
Portagen *(Mead Johnson)*
Pregestimil *(Mead Johnson)*
Prejomin *(Milupa)*
Promod *(Abbott)*
Prosobee *(Mead Johnson)*
Protifar *(Cow & Gate)*
Reabilan *(Roussel)*
Rite-Diet Gluten-Free *(Nutricia)*
Rite-Diet Low Protein *(Nutricia)*
Rite-Diet Low Sodium Bread *(Nutricia)*
Triosorbon *(Merck)*
Tritamyl *(Procea)*
Trufree *(Cantassium)*
Wysoy *(Wyeth)*

(b) Electrolytes and parenteral nutritional supplements

PoM Addamel *(Kabi)*
PoM Addiphos *(Kabi)*
PoM Additrace *(Kabi)*
Alu-Cap *(3M Health Care)*
PoM Aminofusin L Forte *(Merck)*
PoM Aminoplasmal Preps *(Braun)*
PoM Aminoplex Preps *(Geistlich)*
Aminoven 12 *(MCP)*
Cacit *(Norwich Eaton)*
Calcichew *(Shire)*
Calcimax *(Wallace)*
Calcium Resonium *(Sterling Winthrop)*
Chocovite *(Torbet)*
Citrical *(Shire)*
PoM Dextraven 110 *(CP)*
Dextrolyte *(Cow & Gate)*
Dioralyte *(Rorer)*
Electrolade *(Nicholas)*
En-De-Kay Fluotabs *(Stafford-Miller)*
Fluor-A-Day *(Dental Health)*
Fluorigard *(Colgate-Hoyt)*
Fosfor *(Chancellor)*
PoM Freamine III *(Kendall)*
Gluco-Lyte *(Cupal)*
PoM Glucoplex *(Geistlich)*
Glucoven *(MCP)*

PoM Hepanutrin *(Geistlich)*
PoM Intralipid *(Kabi)*
Kay-Cee-L *(Geistlich)*
Kloref *(Cox)*
Leo K *(Leo)*
PoM Limclair *(Sinclair)*
PoM Lipofundin *(Braun)*
PoM Min-I-Jet Calcium Chloride 10% *(IMS)*
PoM Multibionta *(Merck)*
PoM Nephramine *(Boots)*
NU-K *(Consolidated)*
PoM Nutracel *(Baxter)*
Oral-B Fluoride *(Oral-B Labs)*
PoM Ossopan *(Sanofi)*
PoM Ped-EL *(Kabi)*
PoM Perifusin *(Kabi)*
Phosphate *(Sandoz)*
PoM Plasma-Lyte *(Baxter)*
Rehidrat *(Searle)*
Resonium-A *(Sterling Winthrop)*
Sando-K *(Sandoz)*
Sandocal *(Sandoz)*
Slow Sodium *(Ciba)*
Slow-K *(Ciba)*
PoM Solivito N *(Kabi)*
Solvazinc *(Thames)*
PoM Synthamin *(Baxter)*
PoM Synthamix *(Clintec)*
Titralac *(3M Health Care)*
PoM Vamin *(Kabi)*
PoM Vitlipid N *(Kabi)*
PoM Vitrimix KV *(Kabi)*
Z Span Spansule *(SK&F)*
Zincomed *(Medo)*
Zymafluor *(Zyma)*

(c) Anorectics and weight reducing agents

PoM Adifax *(Servier)*
Celevac *(Boehringer Ing.)*
Nilstim *(De Witt)*
PoM Ponderax Pacaps *(Servier)*
Prefil *(Norgine)*

11. Respiratory System

(a) Expectorants, antitussives, mucolytics and decongestants

Cough and cold preparations may contain drugs of the banned narcotic class eg. codeine; and/or stimulant class eg. pseudoephedrine; check carefully

Ammonium Chloride Mixt. *(Unbranded)*
Balm of Gilead Cough Mixture, Pastilles *(Heath & Heather)*
Beecham Coughcaps *(SmithKline Beecham)*

Beecham Hot Lemon, Blackcurrant, Honey & Lemon *(SmithKline Beecham)*

Benylin Chesty Cough Linctus (NOT Mentholated Linctus) *(Warner-Lambert)*

Benylin Children's Cough Linctus *(Warner-Lambert)*

Benylin Dry Cough *(Warner-Lambert)*

Benzoin Tincture Co. *(Unbranded)*

Bronal *(Cupal)*

Bronalin Expectorant Linctus (NOT Dry Cough Elixir) *(Cupal)*

Bronalin Paediatric Cough Syrup *(Cupal)*

Buttercup Syrup *(LRC)*

Copholco *(Fisons CH)*

Copholcoids *(Fisons CH)*

Covonia Mentholated Bronchial Balsam *(Thornton & Ross)*

PoM Dimyril *(Fisons)*

ES Bronchial Mixture *(Torbet)*

Expulin Dry Cough, Paediatric (NOT Expulin) *(Galen)*

PoM Fabrol *Zyma*

PoM Famel Linctus, Expectorant Pastilles (NOT Original) *(Crookes)*

Fennings Lemon Mixture *(Fennings)*

Fisherman's Friend Honey Cough Syrup *(Lofthouse of Fleetwood)*

Flurex Decongestant Inhalant (NOT other preps) *(Cupal)*

Galenphol *(Galen)*

Gregovite C *(Unigreg)*

Guanor *(RP Drugs)*

Hill's Balsam, Expectorant *(Windsor)*

Histalix *(Wallace)*

PoM Isoaminile Linctus *(Unbranded)*

Jackson's Pastilles (NOT Night Cough Pastilles) *(Ernest Jackson)*

Karvol *(Crookes)*

Lem Plus Powders (NOT Capsules) *(Wallis)*

Lemsip Expectorant, Linctus, Chesty Cough (NOT Cold Relief, Junior) *(Reckitt & Colman)*

Lotussin *(Searle)*

Mac, Mac Plus *(SmithKline Beecham)*

Meltus Expectorant, Junior, Honey & Lemon, Baby Meltus (NOT Dry Cough Elixir) *(Cupal)*

Menthol & Eucalyptus Inhalation *(Unbranded)*

Mentholatum Balm, Nasal Inhaler *(The Mentholatum Co)*

PoM Mucodyne *(Rorer)*

Night Nurse Capsules, Liquid *(SmithKline Beecham)*

Olbas Oil *(GR Lane)*

Owbridges Syrup *(Chefaro)*

Pavacol D *(Boehringer Ing.)*

Penetrol *(Crookes)*

Pholcomed-D *(Medo)*

Robitussin Cough Soother, Junior, Expectorant (NOT Expectorant Plus) *(Whitehall)*

Simple Linctus *(Unbranded)*

Snufflebabe *(Pickles)*

Tancolin *(Nicholas)*

Throaties Family Cough Linctus, Pastilles *(Ernest Jackson)*

Tixylix *(Intercare)*

Vapex *(Fisons)*

Vegetable Cough Remover *(Potter's Herbal)*

Venos Preps *(SmithKline Beecham)*

Vicks Expectorant Cough Syrup *(Procter & Gamble)*

Vicks Inhaler *(Procter & Gamble)*

Vicks VapoRub *(Procter & Gamble)*

Visclair *(Sinclair)*

Wigglesworth Cold and Flu Capsules *(Wigglesworth)*

Wright's Vaporizer *(LRC)*

Wright's Vaporizer Fluid *(LRC)*

(b) Bronchospasm relaxants, other anti-asthma drugs

*Oral and parenteral forms of these preparations are banned

PoM Aerolin Autohaler* *(3M Riker)*

PoM Alupent Aerosol* *(Boehringer Ing.)*

PoM Atrovent *(Boehringer Ing.)*

PoM Becloforte *(Allen & Hanburys)*

PoM Becodisks *(Allen & Hanburys)*

PoM Becotide *(Allen & Hanburys)* Biophylline *(Delandale)*

PoM Bricanyl Inhaler* *(Astra)*

PoM Bricanyl Turbohaler* *(Astra)*

PoM Bricanyl Spacer Inhaler* *(Astra)*

PoM Bricanyl Refill Canister* *(Astra)*

PoM Bricanyl Respules* *(Astra)*

PoM Bricanyl Respirator Solution* *(Astra)* Choledyl *(Parke Davis)*

PoM Intal *(Fisons)*

PoM Labophylline *(LAB)* Lasma *(Pharmax)* Neulin SA, Neulin *(3M Health Care)*

PoM Oxivent *(Boehringer Ing.)* Pecram *(Zyma)*

Phyllocontin Continus *(Napp)* Pro-Vent *(Wellcome)*

PoM Pulmadil* *(3M Health Care)*

PoM Pulmicort *(Astra)* Sabidal SR *(Zyma)*

PoM Salbulin Inhaler* *(3M Health Care)*

PoM Salbuvent Inhaler* *(Tillotts)*

PoM Salbuvent Respirator Solution* *(Tillotts)*

PoM Serevent *(Allen & Hanburys)* Slo-Phyllin *(Lipha)* Theo-Dur *(Astra)* Theodrox *(3M Health Care)*

PoM Tilade *(Fisons)* Tixylix *(Intercare)* Uniphyllin Continus *(Napp)*

PoM Ventide* *(Allen & Hanburys)*

PoM Ventodisks* *(Allen & Hanburys)*

PoM Ventolin Inhaler* *(Allen & Hanburys)*

PoM Ventolin Rotacaps* *(Allen & Hanburys)*

PoM Ventolin Respirator Solution* *(Allen & Hanburys)*

PoM Ventolin Nebules* *(Allen & Hanburys)*

PoM Zaditen *(Sandoz)*

(c) Respiratory stimulants

All respiratory stimulants are banned

12. Allergy and Immune System

(a) Antihistamines

Actidil *(Wellcome)*

Afrazine Preps *(Schering-Plough)*

Aller-eze Tablets, Elixir (NOT Aller-eze Plus) *(Intercare)*

Alunex *(Steinhard)*

PoM Clarityn *(Schering-Plough)* Daneral SA *(Hoechst)* Dimotane LA *(Hoechst)* Dimotane Tablets (NOT Dimotane Plus) *(Hoechst)* Dimotane Elixir *(Hoechst)* Dristan Spray (NOT Tablets) *(Whitehall)*

PoM Fabahistin *(Bayer)* Fenostil-Retard *(Zyma)*

PoM Hismanal *(Janssen)* Histryl *(SK&F)* Lergoban *(3M Health Care)* Mentholease *(Warner-Lambert)*

PoM Nalcrom *(Fisons)* Optimine *(Schering-Plough)* Otrivine-Antistin *(Zyma)* Otrivin Hay Fever Formula Nasal Drops *(Ciba)* Penetrol *(Crookes)*

Periactin *(MSD)*
Phenergan *(May & Baker)*
Piriton *(Allen & Hanburys)*
Pollon-eze *(Janssen)*
PoM Primalan *(May & Baker)*
Pro-Actidil *(Wellcome)*
Resiston One Nasal Spray *(Fisons)*
Rynacrom Nasal Spray, Drops, Compound *(Fisons)*
Seldane *(Merrell Dow)*
PoM Semprex *(Calmic)*
Tavegil *(Sandoz)*
Thephorin *(Sinclair)*
PoM Tinset *(Janssen)*
Triludan, Triludan Forte *(Merrell Dow)*
PoM Vallergan *(May & Baker)*
Vicks Sinex *(Procter & Gamble)*
PoM Zaditen *(Sandoz)*
PoM Zirtek *(Allen & Hanburys)*

(b) Anti-allergy preparations

PoM Pharmalgen *(Pharmacia)*
PoM Spectralgen *(Pharmacia)*

(c) Vaccines and immunoglobulins

PoM AC Vax *(SK&F)*
PoM Almevax *(Wellcome)*
PoM Arilvax *(Wellcome)*
PoM Endobulin *(Immuno)*
PoM Engerix B *(SK&F)*
PoM Ervevax *(SK&F)*
PoM Fluvirin *(Servier)*
PoM Gamimune-N *(Cutter)*
PoM Gammabulin *(Immuno)*
PoM Humotet *(Wellcome)*
PoM Immravax *(Merieux)*
PoM Influvac Sub-Unit *(Duphar)*
PoM Kabiglobulin *(Kabi)*
PoM M-M-RII *(Wellcome)*
PoM Mengivac (AC) *(Merieux)*
PoM MFV-Ject *(Merieux)*
PoM Mevilin-L *(Evans)*
PoM Mumpsvax *(Morson)*
PoM Partobulin *(Immuno)*
PoM Pluserix MMR *(SK&F)*
PoM Pneumovax II *(MSD)*
PoM Rubavax *(Merieux)*
PoM Sandoglobulin *(Sandoz)*
PoM Tetavax *(Merieux)*
PoM Trivax *(Wellcome)*

(d) Immunosuppressants

PoM Azamune *(Penn Pharm)*
PoM Berkaprine *(Berk)*
PoM Immunoprin *(Ashbourne)*
PoM Imuran *(Wellcome)*
PoM Pressimmune *(Hoechst)*
PoM Sandimmun *(Sandoz)*

13. Ear, Nose and Oropharynx

(a) Topical otic (ear) medication

PoM Achromycin *(Lederle)*
Audax *(Napp Consumer)*
PoM Audicort *(Lederle)*
Audinorm *(Carlton)*
PoM Betnesol, Betnesol-N *(Glaxo)*
Canesten *(Baypharm)*
Cerumol *(LAB)*
PoM Cidomycin *(Roussel)*
Dioctyl Ear Drops *(Medo)*
Exterol *(Dermal)*
PoM Framycort *(Fisons)*
PoM Framygen *(Fisons)*
PoM Garamycin *(Schering-Plough)*
PoM Genticin *(Nicholas)*
PoM Gentisone HC *(Nicholas)*
PoM Locorten-Vioform *(Zyma)*
Molcer *(Wallace)*
PoM Neo-Cortef *(Upjohn)*
PoM Otomize *(Stafford-Miller)*
PoM Otosporin *(Wellcome)*
PoM Predsol, Predsol-N *(Glaxo)*
PoM Sofradex *(Roussel)*
PoM Terra-Cortril *(Pfizer)*
PoM Tri-Adcortyl Otic *(Princeton)*
PoM Vista-Methasone,
Vista-Methasone N *(Daniels)*
Waxsol *(Norgine)*

(b) Topical nasopharyngeal (nasal) medication

Afrazine *(Schering-Plough)*
PoM Bactroban Nasal *(Beecham)*
PoM Beconase *(Allen & Hanburys)*
PoM Betnesol *(Glaxo)*
PoM Dexa-Rhinaspray *(Boehringer Ing.)*
Dristan Spray (NOT Tablets) *(Whitehall)*
PoM Naseptin *(ICI)*
Otrivine *(Ciba)*
Otrivine Hay Fever Formula Nasal Drops *(Ciba)*
Resiston One Nasal Spray *(Fisons)*
PoM Rhinocort *(Astra)*
PoM Rinatec *(Boehringer Ing.)*
Rynacrom Preps *(Fisons)*
PoM Syntaris *(Syntex)*
Vicks Sinex *(Procter & Gamble)*
PoM Vista-Methasone *(Daniels)*

(c) Topical oropharyngeal (mouth, throat) medication

AAH Throat Spray *(Rorer)*
PoM Adcortyl in Orabase *(Princeton)*

Antiseptic Throat Pastilles *(Ernest Jackson)*
Betadine Gargle and Mouth Wash *(Napp)*
PoM Bioplex *(Thames)*
Bioral *(Sterling Winthrop)*
Bocasan *(Oral-B)*
Bonjela *(Reckitt & Colman)*
Bradosol, Bradosol Plus *(Ciba)*
Calgel *(Wellcome)*
Chloraseptic *(Procter & Gamble)*
PoM Corlan *(Glaxo)*
Corsodyl *(ICI)*
PoM Daktarin Oral Gel *(Janssen)*
Dequacaine *(Crookes)*
Dequacets *(Crookes)*
Dequadin *(Crookes)*
Difflam *(3M Health Care)*
PoM Diflucan *(Pfizer)*
Eludril *(Pierre Fabre)*
PoM Flagyl *(May & Baker)*
PoM Fungilin *(Squibb)*
Glandosane *(Fresenius)*
Jackson's Children's Cough Pastilles *(Ernest Jackson)*
Jackson's Pholcodine Cough Pastilles (NOT Night Cough Pastilles) *(Ernest Jackson)*
Labosept *(LAB)*
PoM Locabiotal *(Servier)*
Mac Extra *(SmithKline Beecham)*
Medilave *(Martindale)*
Meggezones *(Schering-Plough)*
Mentholatum Antiseptic Lozenges *(Mentholatum)*
Mentholease *(Warner-Lambert)*
Merocaine *(Merrell Dow)*
Merocets *(Merrell Dow)*
Merothol *(Merrell Dow)*
PoM Metrolyl *(Lagap)*
Naxogin 500 *(Farmitalia)*
PoM Nystan *(Princeton)*
Orabase *(Squibb)*
Oralcer *(Vitabiotics)*
Oraldene *(Warner-Lambert)*
Penetrol *(Crookes)*
Potter's Pastilles *(Booker)*
Proctor's Pinelyptus Pastilles *(Ernest Jackson)*
Pyralvex *(Norgine)*
Saliva Orthana *(Nycomed)*
Salivix *(Thames)*
Strepsils *(Crookes)*
TCP Pastilles *(Chemist Brokers)*
Teejel *(Napp Consumer)*
Throaties Extra *(Ernest Jackson)*
Tyrocane Throat Lozenges *(Cupal)*
Tyrozets *(MSD)*
Valda Pastilles *(Sterling Health)*
Vicks Chloraseptic Spray *(Procter & Gamble)*

PoM = Prescription-only Medicines

Vocalzone *(English Grains)*
PoM Zadstat *(Lederle)*
Zensyls *(Ernest Jackson)*

14. Eye

(a) Topical ocular anti-infective preparations

PoM Achromycin *(Lederle)*
PoM Albucid *(Nicholas)*
PoM Aureomycin *(Lederle)*
PoM Betnesol-N *(Glaxo)*
Brolene *(Fisons)*
PoM Chloromycetin *(Parke Davis)*
PoM Cidomycin *(Roussel)*
PoM Framygen *(Fisons)*
PoM Fucithalmic *(Leo)*
PoM Garamycin *(Schering-Plough)*
PoM Genticin *(Nicholas)*
PoM Graneodin *(Squibb)*
PoM Idoxene *(Spodefell)*
PoM Kerecid *(Allergan)*
PoM Minims Chloramphenicol *(SNP)*
PoM Minims Gentamicin *(SNP)*
PoM Minims Neomycin *(SNP)*
PoM Minims Sulphacetamide *(SNP)*
PoM Neosporin *(Wellcome)*
PoM Opulets Chloramphenicol *(Alcon)*
PoM Polyfax *(Wellcome)*
PoM Polytrim *(Wellcome)*
PoM Sno Phenicol *(SNP)*
PoM Soframycin *(Roussel)*
PoM Tobralex *(Alcon)*
PoM Zovirax *(Wellcome)*

(b) Topical ocular steroid, anti-inflammatory, preparations

PoM Betnesol, Betnesol-N *(Glaxo)*
Brolene *(Fisons)*
PoM Chloromycetin Hydrocortisone *(Parke Davis)*
PoM Eumovate, Eumovate-N *(Glaxo)*
PoM FML, FML-Neo *(Allergan)*
PoM Framycort *(Fisons)*
Isopro-Frin *(Alcon)*
PoM Maxidex *(Alcon)*
PoM Maxitrol *(Alcon)*
PoM Minims Prednisolone *(SNP)*
PoM Neo-Cortef *(Upjohn)*
PoM Opticrom *(Fisons)*
Otrivine-Antistin *(Zyma)*
PoM Pred Forte *(Allergan)*
PoM Predsol, Predsol-N *(Glaxo)*
PoM Sofradex *(Roussel)*
PoM Tanderil, Tanderil Chloramphenicol *(Zyma)*
PoM Vasocon-A *(Iolab)*
PoM Vista-Methasone, Vista-Methasone N *(Daniels)*

(c) Glaucoma

PoM Ismelin *(Zyma)*
PoM Isopto Carbachol *(Alcon)*
PoM Isopto Carpine *(Alcon)*
PoM Minims Pilocarpine *(SNP)*
PoM Ocusert Pilo *(May & Baker)*
PoM Opulets Pilocarpine *(Alcon)*
PoM Sno Pilo *(SNP)*

(d) Mydriatics, anaesthetics and stains

PoM Isopto Atropine *(Alcon)*
PoM Minims Amethocaine *(SNP)*
PoM Minims Atropine *(SNP)*
PoM Minims Benoxinate *(SNP)*
PoM Minims Cyclopentolate *(SNP)*
Minims Fluorescein *(SNP)*
PoM Minims Homatropine *(SNP)*
PoM Minims Lignocaine and Fluorescein *(SNP)*
Minims Rose Bengal *(SNP)*
PoM Minims Thymoxamine *(SNP)*
PoM Minims Tropicamide *(SNP)*
PoM Mydriacyl *(Alcon)*
PoM Mydrilate *(Boehringer Ing.)*
PoM Ophthaine *(Squibb)*
PoM Opulets Atropine *(Alcon)*
PoM Opulets Benoxinate *(Alcon)*
PoM Opulets Cyclopentolate *(Alcon)*
Opulets Fluorescein *(Alcon)*

(e) Other ophthalmic medication including lubricants

Eye Dew *(Crookes)*
PoM Healonid *(Pharmacia)*
Hypotears *(Iolab)*
PoM Ilube *(DF)*
Isopto Alkaline *(Alcon)*
Isopto Plain *(Alcon)*
Lacri-Lube *(Allergan)*
Liquifilm Tears *(Allergan)*
Minims Artificial Tears *(SNP)*
Minims Castor Oil *(SNP)*
Minims Saline *(SNP)*
PoM Miochol *(Copper Vision)*
Normasol *(Setcn)*
Optrex *(Crookes)*
Opulets Saline *(Alcon)*
Sno Tears *(SNP)*
Tears Naturale *(Alcon)*
Topiclens *(Seton)*
PoM Zonulysin *(Henleys)*

15. Skin

(a) Emollients and anti-pruritics

Alcoderm *(Galderma)*
Alpha Keri *(Westwood)*
Anthisan *(Fisons)*
Aquadrate *(Norwich Eaton)*
Aveeno *(Bioglan)*
Balneum *(Merck)*
Caladryl *(Warner-Lambert)*
Calendolon *(Weleda)*
Calmurid *(Pharmacia)*
PoM Dapsone *(Unbranded)*
Dermalex *(Sanofi)*
Dermidex *(International)*
Diprobase *(Schering-Plough)*
E45 *(Crookes)*
Eczederm *(Quinoderm)*
Emulsiderm *(Dermal)*
PoM Epogam *(Scotia)*
Eurax *(Ciba Consumer)*
Humiderm *(BritCair)*
Hydromol *(Quinoderm)*
Kamillosan *(Norgine)*
Keri *(Westwood)*
Lacticare *(Steifel)*
Lipobase *(Brocades)*
Locobase *(Brocades)*
Masse *(Cilag)*
Metanium *(Chancellor)*
Miol *(BritCair)*
Morhulin *(Napp Consumer)*
Morsep *(Napp Consumer)*
Natuderm *(Leo)*
Noratex *(Norton)*
Nupercainal *(Ciba)*
Nutraplus *(Galderma)*
Oilatum Emollient *(Stiefel)*
Orabase *(Squibb Surgicare)*
Orahesive *(Squibb Surgicare)*
PoM Parfenac *(Lederle)*
R.B.C. *(Rybar)*
Rikospray Balsam *(3M Health Care)*
Rikospray Silicone *(3M Health Care)*
Sential E *(Pharmacia)*
Siopel *(ICI)*
Solarcaine *(Schering-Plough)*
Sprilon *(Pharmacia)*
Sudocrem *(Tosara)*
Thovaline *(Ilon)*
Ultrabase *(Schering HC)*
Unguentum *(Merck)*
Vasogen *(Pharmax)*

(b) Topical antifungals, antibacterials and disinfectants

PoM Achromycin *(Lederle)*
Anaflex *(Geistlich)*
Aquasept *(Hough, Hoseason)*
PoM Aureomycin *(Lederle)*
Bacticlens *(Seton)*
Bactrian *(Loveridge)*
PoM Bactroban *(Beecham)*
Betadine Preps *(Napp)*
Brulidine *(Fisons)*
PoM Canesten *(Baypharm)*

PoM Cetavlex *(ICI)*
Cetavlon *(ICI)*
Cetriclens *(Seton)*
PoM Chlorasept *(Baxter)*
PoM Cicatrin *(Wellcome)*
PoM Cidomycin *(Roussel)*
Conotrane *(Boehringer Ing.)*
CX Powder *(Seton)*
Daktarin *(Janssen)*
Disadine D.P. *(Stuart)*
Drapolene *(Wellcome)*
Ecostatin *(Princeton)*
PoM Exelderm *(ICI)*
PoM Flamazine *(SNP)*
PoM Framygen *(Fisons)*
PoM Fucidin *(Leo)*
PoM Genticin *(Nicholas)*
PoM Graneodin *(Squibb)*
Hibiscrub *(ICI)*
Hibidil *(ICI)*
Hibisol *(ICI)*
Hibitane *(ICI)*
Hioxyl *(Quinoderm)*
Lamasil *(Sandoz)*
Malatex *(Norton)*
Manusept *(Hough, Hoseason)*
Monphytol *(LAB)*
Mycil *(Crookes)*
Mycota *(Crookes)*
PoM Nizoral *(Janssen)*
Normasol *(Seton)*
PoM Nystaform *(Bayer)*
PoM Nystan *(Princeton)*
Permitabs *(Bioglan)*
Pevaryl *(Cilag)*
pHiso-Med *(Sterling Winthrop)*
Phytex *(Pharmax)*
Phytocil *(Fisons CH)*
PoM Pimafucin *(Brocades)*
PoM Polybactrin *(Wellcome)*
PoM Polyfax *(Wellcome)*
Quinoped *(Quinoderm)*
Roccal *(Sterling Winthrop)*
Rotersept *(Roterpharma)*
Savoclens *(ICI)*
Savlodil *(ICI)*
Savlon Hospital Conc. *(ICI)*
PoM Soframycin *(Roussel)*
PoM Sporanox *(Janssen)*
Ster-Zac Bath Conc. *(Hough, Hoseason)*
PoM Ster-Zac D.C. *(Hough, Hoseason)*
Ster-Zac Powder *(Hough, Hoseason)*
Timoped *(Reckitt & Colman)*
PoM Tinaderm-M *(Schering-Plough)*
Tineafax *(Wellcome)*
Tisept *(Seton)*
Topiclens *(Seton)*
Travasept 100 *(Baxter)*
PoM Tribiotic *(3M Health Care)*
Triclosept *(Hough, Hoseason)*
PoM Trosyl *(Novex)*
Unisept *(Seton)*

Valpeda *(Roche)*
Vesagex *(Rybar)*
Videne *(3M Health Care)*

(c) Scabicides and pediculicides

Ascabiol *(May & Baker)*
Carylderm *(Napp Consumer)*
Clinicide *(De Witt)*
Derbac Shampoo *International*
Derbac-M *(International)*
Eurax *(Ciba Consumer)*
Full Marks *(Napp Consumer)*
Lyclear *(Wellcome)*
Prioderm *(Napp Consumer)*
Quellada *(Stafford-Miller)*
Suleo-C *(International)*
Suleo-M *(International)*
Tetmosol *(ICI)*

(d) Psoriasis, seborrhoea and ichthyosis

Alphosyl *(Stafford-Miller)*
PoM Anthranol *(Stiefel)*
PoM Antraderm *(Brocades)*
Balneum with Tar *(Merck)*
Baltar *(Merck)*
Betadine Scalp and Skin Cleanser, Shampoo *(Napp)*
Capasal *(Dermal)*
Capitol *(Dermal)*
Carbo-Dome *(Lagap)*
Ceanel Conc. *(Quinoderm)*
Clinitar Cream *(SNP)*
Cocois *(Bioglan)*
Cradocap *(Napp Consumer)*
Dithrocream *(Dermal)*
Dithrolan *(Dermal)*
PoM Efalith *(Scotia)*
Exolan *(Dermal)*
Gelcosal *(Quinoderm)*
Gelcotar *(Quinoderm)*
Genisol *(Fisons)*
Ionil T *(Galderma)*
Lenium *(Janssen)*
PoM Nizoral Shampoo *(Janssen)*
Polytar Preps *(Stiefel)*
Pragmatar *(Bioglan)*
Psoradrate *(Norwich Eaton)*
Psoriderm *(Dermal)*
Psorigel *(Galderma)*
Psorin *(Thames)*
Selsun *(Abbott)*
Synogist *(Townendale)*
T Gel *(Neutrogena)*
PoM Tigason *(Roche)*

(e) Acne treatments

Acetoxyl *(Stiefel)*
Acnegel *(Stiefel)*
Acnidazil *(Janssen)*
PoM Actinac *(Roussel)*
Benoxyl *(Stiefel)*

Benzagel *(Bioglan)*
Brasivol *(Stiefel)*
Clearasil *(Procter & Gamble)*
PoM Dalacin T *(Upjohn)*
PoM Dianette *(Schering HC)*
Eskamel *(SK&F)*
Ionax *(Galderma)*
PoM Minocin 50 *(Lederle)*
Nericur *(Schering HC)*
Oxy *(SmithKline Beecham)*
Panoxyl *(Stiefel)*
Quinoderm Preps *(Quinoderm)*
PoM Retin-A *(Cilag)*
PoM Roaccutane *(Roche)*
PoM Stiemycin *(Stiefel)*
PoM Topicycline *(Norwich Eaton)*
Torbetol *(Torbet)*
PoM Vibramycin 50 *(Invicta)*
PoM Zineryt *(Brocades)*

(f) Wart removers

Callusolve *(Dermal)*
Cuplex *(SNP)*
Duofilm *(Stiefel)*
Glutarol *(Dermal)*
Novaruca *(Bioglan)*
Posalfilin *(Norgine)*
Salactol *(Dermal)*
Salatac *(Dermal)*
Veracur *(Typharm)*
Verrugon *(Pickles)*
Verucasep *(Galen)*

(g) Leg ulcer treatments

Aserbine *(Bencard)*
Betadine *(Napp)*
Chlorasol *(Seton)*
Debrisan *(Pharmacia)*
PoM Flamazine *(SNP)*
Hioxyl *(Quinoderm)*
PoM Iodosorb *(Perstorp)*
Paroven *(Zyma)*
PoM Variclene *(Dermal)*
PoM Varidase *(Lederle)*
Vita-E *(Bioglan)*

(h) Topical corticosteroids

PoM Adcortyl *(Princeton)*
PoM Alphaderm *(Norwich Eaton)*
PoM Alphosyl HC *(Stafford-Miller)*
PoM Aureocort *(Lederle)*
PoM Barquinol HC *(Fisons)*
PoM Betnovate Preps (topical use on skin only) *(Glaxo)*
PoM Calmurid HC *(Pharmacia)*
PoM Canesten-HC *(Bayer)*
PoM Carbo-Cort *(Lagap)*
PoM Cobadex *(Cox)*
PoM Daktacort *(Janssen)*
PoM Dermovate Preps *(Glaxo)*
PoM Dioderm *(Dermal)*
PoM Diprosalic *(Schering-Plough)*
PoM Diprosone *(Schering-Plough)*

PoM Econacort *(Princeton)*
PoM Efcortelan *(Glaxo)*
PoM Epifoam *(Stafford-Miller)*
PoM Eumovate *(Glaxo)*
PoM Eurax-Hydrocortisone *(Zyma)*
PoM Framycort *(Fisons)*
PoM Fucibet *(Leo)*
PoM Fucidin H *(Leo)*
PoM Genticin HC *(Nicholas)*
PoM Gregoderm *(Unigreg)*
PoM Haelan Preps *(Dista)*
PoM Halciderm *(Squibb)*
PoM Hydrocal *(Bioglan)*
PoM Hydrocortistab *(Boots)*
PoM Hydrocortisyl *(Roussel)* .
PoM Ledercort *(Lederle)*
PoM Locoid *(Brocades)*
PoM Lotriderm *(Schering-Plough)*
PoM Metosyn *(Stuart)*
PoM Mildison Lipocream *(Brocades)*
PoM Modrasone *(Schering-Plough)*
PoM Neo-Medrone Cream *(Upjohn)*
PoM Nerisone *(Schering HC)*
PoM Nystadermal *(Princeton)*
PoM Nystaform-HC *(Bayer)*
PoM Pevaryl TC *(Cilag)*
PoM Preferid *(Brocades)*
PoM Propaderm *(Glaxo)*
PoM Quinocort *(Quinoderm)*
PoM Sential *(Pharmacia)*
PoM Stiedex *(Stiefel)*
PoM Synalar *(ICI)*
PoM Tarcortin *(Stafford-Miller)*
PoM Terra-Cortril *(Pfizer)*
PoM Timodine *(Lloyds)*
PoM Topilar *(Bioglan)*
PoM Tri-Adcortyl *(Princeton)*
PoM Tri-Cicatrin *(Wellcome)*
PoM Tridesilon *(Lagap)*
PoM Trimovate *(Glaxo)*
PoM Ultradil *(Schering HC)*
PoM Ultralanum *(Schering HC)*
PoM Vioform-Hydrocortisone *(Zyma)*

(i) Other dermatological preparations

Almay Total Sunbloc *(Almay)*
PoM Anhydrol Forte *(Dermal)*
Atmocol *(Thackray)*
Boots Covering Cream *(Boots)*
Chironair *(Downs)*
Comfeel *(Coloplast)*
Coppertone Preps *(Scholl)*
Covermark *(Stiefel)*
Dermacolor *(Fox)*
Dor *(Simpla)*
PoM Driclor *(Stiefel)*
Hirudoid *(Panpharma)*
Hyperdrol *(BritCair)*
Keromask *(Innoxa)*
Lasonil *(Bayer)*
Limone *(CliniMed)*
Nilodor *(Loxley Medical)*
No Roma *(Salt)*

Ostobon *(Coloplast)*
Piz Buin Preps *(Ciba)*
PoM Regaine *(Upjohn)*
RoC Total Sunblock *(RoC)*
Secaderm *(Fisons)*
Spectraban 15 *(Stiefel)*
Stomogel *(Thackray)*
Translet Preps *(Franklin Med)*
Uvistat *(Windsor)*
Veil Cover Cream *(Blake)*
Zeasorb *(Stiefel)*

16. Surgical Preparations

Plain anaesthetic preparations are permitted (when medically justified), those with adrenaline are not

Written notification must be submitted immediately to the IOC Medical Commission

(a) Anaesthetics, muscle relaxants and premeds

PoM Add-A-Med Thiopentone Sodium *(IMS)*
PoM Alloferin *(Roche)*
PoM Anectine *(Wellcome)*
Anethaine *(Crookes)*
PoM Anexate *(Roche)*
PoM Ativan *(Wyeth)*
PoM Brietal Sodium *(Lilly)*
PoM Citanest *(Astra)*
PoM Diazemuls *(Dumex)*
PoM Diprivan *(ICI)*
PoM EMLA *(Astra)*
PoM Flaxedil *(May & Baker)*
Fluothane *(ICI)*
Forane *(Abbott)*
PoM Hypnomidate *(Janssen)*
PoM Hypnovel *(Roche)*
PoM Intraval Sodium *(May & Baker)*
PoM Jexin *(DF)*
PoM Ketalar *(Parke Davis)*
PoM Marcain Steripack *(Astra)*
Nitrous Oxide *(Unbranded)*
PoM Norcuron *(Organon Teknika)*
PoM Normison *(Wyeth)*
PoM Pavulon *(Organon Teknika)*
PoM Robinul *(Wyeth)*
PoM Scoline *(DF)*
PoM Stesolid *(CP Pharm)*
PoM Tensilon *(Roche)*
PoM Tracrium *(Calmic)*
PoM Transiderm-Nitro *(Ciba)*
PoM Tubarine *(Wellcome)*
PoM Valium *(Roche)*
PoM Vallergan *(May & Baker)*
Xylocaine Spray *(Astra)*

(b) Plasma products

Albuminar Preps *(Armour)*
Buminate *(Baxter)*

PoM Demser *(MSD)*
PoM Gelofusine *(Consolidated)*
PoM Gentran Preps *(Baxter)*
PoM Haemaccel *(Hoechst)*
PoM Lomodex Preps *(CP)*
PoM Macrodex *(Pharmacia)*
PoM Rheomacrodex *(Pharmacia)*
PoM STD *(STD Pharm)*

17. Diagnostic Agents

Acetest *(Ames)*
Albustix *(Ames)*
Albym Test *(BM Diag)*
BM-Test 1-44 *(BM Diag)*
Clinistix *(Ames)*
Clinitest *(Ames)*
Dextrostix *(Ames)*
Diabur-Test 5000 *(BM Pharm)*
Diastix *(Ames)*
Exactech *(Medisense)*
Glucostix *(Ames)*
Hypoguard GA *(Hypoguard)*
Ketostix *(Ames)*
Ketur Test *(BM Diag)*
PoM Metopirone *(Ciba)*
Phenistix *(Ames)*

18. Contraceptive Agents

(a) Oral contraceptives

PoM Binovum *(Ortho)*
PoM Brevinor *(Syntex)*
PoM Conova 30 *(Gold Cross)*
PoM Eugynon 30 *(Schering HC)*
PoM Femodene *(Schering HC)*
PoM Femodene ED *(Schering HC)*
PoM Femulen *(Gold Cross)*
PoM Loestrin 20, Loestrin 30 *(Parke Davis)*
PoM Logynon *(Schering HC)*
PoM Logynon ED *(Schering HC)*
PoM Marvelon *(Organon)*
PoM Mercilon *(Organon)*
PoM Microgynon 30 *(Schering HC)*
PoM Micronor *(Ortho)*
PoM Microval *(Wyeth)*
PoM Minulet *(Wyeth)*
PoM Neocon 1/35 *(Ortho)*
PoM Neogest *(Schering HC)*
PoM Norgeston *(Schering HC)*
PoM Noriday *(Syntex)*
PoM Norimin *(Syntex)*
PoM Norinyl-1 *(Syntex)*
PoM Ortho-Novin 1/50 *(Ortho)*
PoM Ovran, Ovran 30 *(Wyeth)*
PoM Ovranette *(Wyeth)*
PoM Ovysmen *(Ortho)*
PoM Schering PC4 *(Schering HC)*
PoM Synphase *(Syntex)*
PoM Trinordiol *(Wyeth)*
PoM Trinovum *(Ortho)*

(b) Spermicidal contraceptives

C-Film *(De Witt)*
Delfen *(Ortho)*
Double Check *(FPS)*
Duracreme *(LRC)*
Duragel *(LRC)*
Gynol II *(Ortho)*
Ortho-Creme *(Ortho)*
Ortho-Forms *(Ortho)*
Ortho-Gynol *(Ortho)*
Staycept *(Syntex)*

(c) Depot contraceptives

PoM Depo-Provera *(Upjohn)*
PoM Noristerat *(Schering HC)*

(d) Contraceptive devices

Cap, Contraceptive
(Unbranded)
Contraceptive sheath/condom
(Various)
Diaphragm, Contraceptive
(Unbranded)
Dumas *(Lamberts)*
Durex Flat Spring Diaphragm
(LRC)
Fertility Thermometer
(Unbranded)
PoM Gravigard *(Gold Cross)*
Intrauterine Devices
(Unbranded)
PoM Multiload Cu 250, 250 Short,
375 *(Organon)*
PoM Nova-T *(Schering HC)*
PoM Novagard *(Kabi)*
Ortho Diaphragm *(Ortho)*
Ortho-Gyne T, 380S *(Ortho)*
Prentif *(Lamberts)*
Thermometer, Fertility
(Unbranded)
Vimule *(Lamberts)*

19. Miscellaneous

(a) Detoxifying agents, antidotes

PoM Antabuse *(CP Pharm)*
Carbomix *(Penn Pharm)*
PoM Desferal *(Ciba)*
PoM Digibind *(Wellcome)*
PoM Distamine *(Dista)*
PoM Kelocyanor *(Lipha)*
PoM Ledclair *(Sinclair)*
Medicoal *(Torbet)*
PoM Min-I-Jet Naloxone *(IMS)*
PoM Nalorex *(Du Pont)*
PoM Narcan *(Du Pont)*
Nicorette *(Lundbeck)*
PoM Nicorette Plus *(Lundbeck)*

PoM Parvolex *(DF)*
PoM Pendramine *(Degussa)*
PoM Refolinon *(Farmitalia)*

(b) Cholinergic, anticholinergic and other agents

PoM Mestinon *(Roche)*
PoM Metopirone *(Ciba)*
PoM Prostigmin *(Roche)*
PoM Tensilon *(Roche)*
PoM Ubretid *(Rorer)*

20. Vitamins and Minerals

(a) Vitamins and minerals

AT 10 *(Sterling Winthrop)*
Abidec *(Warner-Lambert)*
Allbee with C *(Whitehall)*
BC 500 *(Wyeth)*
Becosym *(Roche)*
Benadon *(Roche)*
Benerva *(Roche)*
Children's Vitamin Drops
(Hough)
PoM Cobalin-H *(Paines & Byrne)*
Comploment Continus *(Napp)*
Concavit *(Wallace)*
Cytacon *(DF)*
PoM Cytamen *(DF)*
Dalivit *(Paines & Byrne)*
Ephynal *(Roche)*
Forceval *(Unigreg)*
Gregovite C Tablets *(Unigreg)*
Halycitrol *(LAB)*
PoM Ketovite *(Paines & Byrne)*
Lipoflavonoid *(Lipomed)*
Lipotriad *(Lipomed)*
Minamino *(Chancellor)*
Multivite *(DF)*
PoM Neo-Cytamen *(DF)*
Octovit *(SK&F)*
PoM One-Alpha *(Leo)*
Orovite *(Bencard)*
Orovite 7 *(Bencard)*
PoM Parentrovite *(Bencard)*
Paxadon *(Mercury)*
Pharmaton *(Unichem)*
PoM Potaba *(Glenwood)*
PoM Pyridoxine *(Unbranded)*
Redoxon *(Roche)*
Refolinon *(Farmitalia)*
PoM Ro-A-Vit *(Roche)*
PoM Rocaltrol *(Roche)*
Sanatogen Preps *(Fisons)*
Seven Seas Preps *(Seven
Seas)*
Surbex T *(Abbott)*
Tachyrol *(Duphar)*
Vigranon B *(Wallace Mfg)*

(b) Tonics

Effico [NB. Contains caffeine]
(Pharmax)
Gentian Mixture, Acid, Alkaline
(Unbranded)
Glykola [NB. Contains caffeine
and kola] *(Sinclair)*
Koladex [NB. Contains caffeine
and kola] *(LAB)*
Labiton [NB. Contains caffeine]
(LAB)
Metatone *(Warner Lambert)*
Minadex Tonic *(Seven Seas)*
Periactin *(MSD)*
Phyllosan *(SmithKline
Beecham)*
X89 Geriomar *(Pan American)*

PoM = Prescription-only Medicines